Being Fair
and Honest

Character Education

Character Education

Being Fair and Honest

TARA TOMCZYK KOELLHOFFER

INTRODUCTION BY CONSULTING EDITORS
Madonna M. Murphy, Ph.D.
University of St. Francis
and **Sharon L. Banas**
former Values Education Coordinator,
Sweet Home Central School District, New York

CHELSEA HOUSE
PUBLISHERS
An imprint of Infobase Publishing

Character Education: Being Fair and Honest

Copyright © 2009 by Infobase Publishing

Chelsea House
An imprint of Infobase Publishing
132 West 31st Street
New York NY 10001

Library of Congress Cataloging-in-Publication Data
Koellhoffer, Tara Tomczyk.
  Being fair and honest / Tara Koellhoffer.
    p. cm.—(Character education)
  Includes bibliographical references and index.
  ISBN 978-1-60413-118-5 (hardcover)
  1. Fairness. 2. Honesty. I. Title. II. Series.
BJ1533.F2K64 2009
  179'.9—dc22   2008025307

Chelsea House books are available at special discounts when purchased in bulk quantities for businesses, associations, institutions, or sales promotions. Please call our Special Sales Department in New York at (212) 967-8800 or (800) 322-8755.

You can find Chelsea House on the World Wide Web
at http://www.chelseahouse.com

Text design by Annie O'Donnell
Cover design by Takeshi Takahashi

Printed in the United States

Bang NMSG 10 9 8 7 6 5 4 3 2 1

This book is printed on acid-free paper.

All links and Web addresses were checked and verified to be correct at the time of publication. Because of the dynamic nature of the Web, some addresses and links may have changed since publication and may no longer be valid.

CONTENTS

INTRODUCTION

On February 14, 2008, as these books were being edited, a shooting occurred at Northern Illinois University (NIU) in DeKalb, Illinois. A former NIU graduate student, dressed in black and armed with a shotgun and two handguns, opened fire from the stage of a lecture hall. The shooter killed five students and injured 16 others before committing suicide. What could have led someone to do this? Could it have been prevented?

When the shooting started, student Dan Parmenter and his girlfriend, Lauren Debrauwere, who was sitting next to him, dropped to the floor between the rows of seats. Dan covered Lauren with his body, held her hand, and began praying. The shield of Dan's body saved Lauren's life, but Dan was fatally wounded. In that hall, on February 14, 2008—Valentine's Day—one person's deed was horrific and filled with hate; another's was heroic and loving.

The purpose of this series of books is to help prevent the occurrence of this kind of violence by offering readers the character education and social and emotional skills they need to control their emotions and make good moral choices. This series includes books on topics such as coping with bullying, conflicts, peer pressure, prejudice, anger and frustration, and numerous responsibilities, as well as learning how to handle teamwork and respect for others, be fair and honest, and be a good leader and decision-maker.

In his 1992 book, *Why Johnny Can't Tell Right from Wrong,*[1] William Kilpatrick coined the term "moral illiteracy" and dedicated a whole chapter to it. Today, as he points out, people often do not recognize when they are in a situation that calls for a moral choice, and they are not able to define what is right and what is wrong in that situation. The California-based Josephson Institute of Ethics agrees with these concerns. The institute states that we have a "character deficit" in our society today and points out that increasing numbers of young people across the United States—from well-to-do as well as disadvantaged backgrounds—demonstrate reckless disregard for fundamental standards of ethical conduct.

According to the 2006 *Josephson Institute Report Card on the Ethics of American Youth*, our children are at risk. This report sets forth the results of a biannual written survey completed in 2006 by more than 36,000 high school students across the country. The compilers of the report found that 82 percent of the students surveyed admitted that they had lied to a parent about something significant within the previous year. Sixty percent admitted to having cheated during a test at school, and 28 percent admitted to having stolen something from a store.[2] (Various books in this series will tell of other findings in this report.) Clearly, helping young people to develop character is a need of national importance.

The United States Congress agrees. In 1994, in the joint resolution that established National Character Counts Week, Congress declared that "the character of a nation is only as strong as the character of its individual citizens." The resolution also stated that "people do not automatically develop good character and, therefore, conscientious efforts must be made by youth-influencing institutions . . . to help young people develop the essential traits and characteristics that comprise good character."[3]

Many stories can be told of people who have defended our nation with character. One of the editors of this series knew one such young man named Jason Dunham. On April 24, 2004, Corporal Jason L. Dunham was serving with the United States Marines in Iraq. As Corporal Dunham's squad was conducting a reconnaissance mission, the men heard sounds of rocket-propelled grenades and small arms fire. Corporal

Dunham led a team of men toward that fire to assist their battalion commander's ambushed convoy. An insurgent leaped out at Corporal Dunham, and he saw the man release a grenade. Corporal Dunham alerted his team and immediately covered the grenade with his helmet and his body. He lost his own life, but he saved the lives of others on his team.

In January 2007, the Dunham family traveled to Washington, D.C., where President George W. Bush presented them with Corporal Dunham's posthumously awarded Congressional Medal of Honor. In the words of the Medal of Honor citation, "By his undaunted courage, intrepid fighting spirit, and unwavering devotion to duty, Corporal Dunham gallantly gave his life for his country."[4]

Thomas Lickona, the author of several books including *Educating for Character* and *Character Matters*, explains that the premise of character education is that there are objectively good human qualities—virtues—that are enduring moral truths. Courage, fortitude, integrity, caring, citizenship, and trustworthiness are just a few examples. These moral truths transcend religious, cultural, and social differences and help us to distinguish right from wrong. They are rooted in our human nature. They tell us how we should act with other human beings to promote human dignity and build a well-functioning and civil society—a society in which everyone lives by the golden rule.[5]

To develop his or her character, a person must understand core virtues, care about them, and act upon them. This series of books aims to help young readers *want* to become people of character. The books will help young people understand such core ethical values as fairness, honesty, responsibility, respect, tolerance of others, fortitude, self-discipline, teamwork, and leadership. By offering examples of people today and notable figures in history who live and have lived these virtues, these books will inspire young readers to develop these traits in themselves.

Finally, through these books, young readers will see that if they act on these moral truths, they will make good choices.

They will be able to deal with frustration and anger, manage conflict resolution, overcome prejudice, handle peer pressure, and deal with bullying. The result, one hopes, will be middle schools, high schools, and neighborhoods in which young people care about one another and work with their class-mates and neighbors to develop team spirit.

Character development is a lifelong task but an exciting challenge. The need for it has been with us since the begin-ning of civilization. As the ancient Greek philosopher Aristo-tle explained in his *Nicomachean Ethics*:

> The virtues we get by first exercising them . . . so too we become just by doing just acts, temperate by doing tem-perate acts, brave by doing brave acts. . . . Hence also it is no easy task to be good . . . to do this to the right person, to the right extent, at the right time, with the right motive, and in the right way, that is not easy; wherefore goodness is both rare and laudable and noble. . . . It makes no small difference, then, whether we form habits of one kind or of another from our very youth; it makes a very great differ-ence, or rather all the difference.[6]

This development of one's character is truly *The Ultimate Gift* that we hope to give to our young people. In the movie version of Jim Stovall's book of the same name, a privileged young man receives a most unexpected inheritance from his grandfather. Instead of the sizeable inheritance of cash that he expects, the young man receives 12 tasks—or "gifts"—designed to challenge him on a journey of self-discovery. The gifts confront him with character choices that force him to decide how one can be truly happy. Is it the possession of money that brings us happiness, or is it what we do with the money that we have? Every one of us has been given gifts. Will we keep our gifts to ourselves, or will we share them with others?

Being a "person of character" can have multiple meanings. Psychologist Steven Pinker asks an interesting question in a

January 13, 2008, *New York Times Magazine* article titled "The Moral Instinct": "Which of the following people would you say is the most admirable: Mother Teresa, Bill Gates, or Norman Borlaug?" Pinker goes on to explain that although most people would say that, of course, Mother Teresa is the most admirable—a true person of character who ministered to the poor in Calcutta, was awarded the Noble Peace Prize, and was ranked in an American poll as the most admired person in the twentieth century—each of these three is a morally admirable person.

Pinker points out that Bill Gates made billions through his company Microsoft, but he also has decided to give away billions of dollars to help alleviate human misery in the United States and around the world. His charitable foundation is built on the principles that "All lives—no matter where they are being lived—have equal value" and "To whom much is given, much is expected."

Pinker notes that very few people have heard of Norman Borlaug, an agronomist who has spent his life developing high-yielding varieties of crops for third world countries. He is known as the "Father of the Green Revolution" because he used agricultural science to reduce world hunger and, by doing so, saved more than a billion lives. Borlaug is one of only five people in history to have won the Nobel Peace Prize, the Presidential Medal of Freedom, and the Congressional Gold Medal. He has devoted his long professional life and his scientific expertise to making the world a better place.

All of these people—although very different, from different places, and with different gifts—are people of character. They are, says Pinker, people with "a sixth sense, the moral sense." It is the sense of trying to do good in whatever situation one finds oneself.[7]

The authors and editors of the series *Character Education* hope that these books will help young readers discover their gifts and develop them, guided by a moral compass. "Do good and avoid evil." "Become all that you can be—a person of character." The books in this series teach these things and more. These books will correlate well with national social studies standards of learning. They will help teachers meet state standards for teaching social and emotional skills, as well as state guidelines for teaching ethics and character education.

Madonna M. Murphy, Ph.D.
Author of *Character Education in America's Blue Ribbon Schools* and professor of education, University of St. Francis, Joliet, Illinois

Sharon L. Banas, M.Ed.
Author of *Caring Messages for the School Year* and former character education coordinator and middle school social studies teacher, Sweet Home Central School District, Amherst and Tonawanda, New York

FOOTNOTES

1. William Kilpatrick. *Why Johnny Can't Tell Right from Wrong,* New York: Simon and Schuster, 1992.
2. Josephson Institute, 2006 *Josephson Institute Report Card on the Ethics of American Youth: Part One – Integrity.* Available online at: http://josephsoninstitute.org/pdf/ReportCard_press-release_2006-1013.pdf.
3. House Joint Resolution 366. May 11, 1994, 103rd Congress. 2d Session.
4. U.S. Army Center of Military History. *The Medal of Honor.* Available online at: www.history.army.mil/moh.html
5. Thomas Lickona, *Educating for Character: Teaching Respect and Responsibility in the Schools.* New York: Bantam, 1991. Thomas Lickona, *Character Matters: How to Help Our Children Develop Good Judgment, Integrity, and Other Essential Virtues.* New York: Simon and Schuster Touchstone Books, 2004.
6. Richard McKeon, editor, "Nicomachean Ethics." *Basic Works of Aristotle,* Chicago: Random House, Clarendon Press, 1941.
7. Steven Pinker, "The Moral Instinct," *The New York Times*, January 13, 2008. Available online at www.newyorktimes.com.

WHAT IS FAIRNESS?

1

Fairness is not an attitude. It's a professional skill that must be developed and exercised.

—Brit Hume (1943–), FOX News anchor

From the time we are small children, we are told that we have to be fair. Our parents tell us to play games by the rules, share our belongings with others, and treat people the way we would like to be treated ourselves. We all have an inherent sense of what fairness means: To be fair means that we behave in a way that is just. We do not favor one person over another. We wait patiently for our turn in a game or in a line. We tell the truth, and we do not take sides with people just because they are our friends—in other words, we are impartial. We strive to do what is right, regardless of the situation. All of these kinds of behaviors are a part of fairness, but there are many other ways to be fair.

JUSTICE

In general, when we talk about fairness, we are talking about interactions among individual people. When we apply the concept of fairness to society as a whole, that is justice. Justice is a cardinal virtue from the time of the Greeks, and it is important to define it correctly if you are going to refer to it. Justice means to give what is owed to another, an individual, or a community. Justice makes it necessary to respect the rights of each person and to establish in relationships a harmony that protects equity with regard to others and the common good. Justice means keeping society in order by giving out rewards and punishments in a fair way and by remaining neutral in arguments between opposing people or groups to help them come to a solution that will satisfy both sides. Justice also means living up to an ideal of the way a good and fair society should be. As Russian writer Alexander Solzhenitsyn put it, "Justice is . . . the conscience of the whole of humanity."

A big part of justice is social justice. This term refers to distributing goods and resources among members of society in a fair way. For centuries, philosophers have debated the best way to bring about social justice. Some, like the communists, believe that government, or the state, should own all business and property, and distribute them to people according to their needs and their ability to work to contribute to the economy and society. Capitalists, on the other hand, believe that individuals have the right to work for and own property, and have the right to choose what to do with that property. They may share it freely with others or charge a fee for its use, or they may donate what they have to people who have less. Socialists generally believe in a mix of communism and capitalism—arguing that key industries, such as health care, and other major property should be controlled by the state, while the people retain the right to own some forms of property, such as land.

Social justice can also be defined in another way: as a system that seeks to create fairness in the social arena, as opposed to in the judicial arena (the courts) and the interpersonal arena (between individuals and groups). In this sense, social justice promotes equality among all people. The goal of social justice is to eliminate poverty, racism, sexism, and other forms of prejudice, and to make all members of society truly

Although "fairness" is a concept that goes back to the earliest humans, a formal system of justice is earliest associated with ancient Greece. In this drawing from *The Story of Greece* by Mary Macgregor, Greek lawmaker Solon is shown giving the order to free a slave, around 595 B.C.

equal. Many people also argue that social justice involves protecting the environment from dangers such as pollution and global warming, which will allow future generations to enjoy the planet just as we do today.

HUMAN EQUALITY

Although the ideal of human equality is considered a part of social justice, it is such an important concept that it can be viewed as a facet, or aspect, of fairness in its own right. The U.S. Declaration of Independence states, "We hold these truths to be self-evident, that all men are created equal, that they are endowed by their Creator with certain unalienable Rights, that among these are Life, Liberty, and the Pursuit of Happiness." Americans (and citizens of most other democratic nations) believe that all people are equal and should be treated that way. We try to create a government and a society that treats all people in the same way, without favoring or having a negative bias against any particular groups or individuals because of factors such as race, gender, or ethnic origin. The ideal of equality forms the basis for a democratic society. The problem is that people are *not* equal, at least not in the sense that they are all exactly the same.

For as long as democracies such as the United States have existed, they have struggled with the question of how to treat people as equals when there are, in fact, huge differences among individuals. Some people are smarter than others; some people are stronger or more athletic; some people have physical or mental disabilities; and some people are born into families that are wealthy, while others are born into poor socioeconomic circumstances. With all these differences between us, how can society possibly treat us all equally?

The concept of equality does not require all people to be treated as if they were the same. Instead, equality, as part of fairness, requires that all people have equal *access* to the same rights, privileges, and opportunities. For example, in the United States, all people have the right to attend public school, free of cost, which (at least in theory) provides everyone with the same opportunities to grow and learn.

Equality also emphasizes the fact that everyone is unique, and that we should tolerate or even celebrate that uniqueness. At the same time, we should ensure that all people have the opportunity to seek happiness for themselves without having to overcome obstacles based on their race, gender, religion, socioeconomic class, or ethnicity.

TOLERANCE

Another concept of fairness, one that is closely tied to the idea of human equality, is tolerance. Ever since the civil rights movement began in the 1950s and 1960s, the word *tolerance* has been a popular one.

To be tolerant means that you accept other people, regardless of their race, religion, gender, class, cultural background, abilities or disabilities, or any other characteristic. Tolerance means seeking to understand and respect people who are different from you and recognizing that all people have the right to exist and to have an equal place in society. Even if you do not agree with their point of view, religion, or some other trait, you show sympathy for their beliefs and refuse to let prejudice guide your actions. Tolerant people are open to new ideas, are willing to learn from others, and reject stereotypes about various groups of people.

Generally, people who are intolerant of those who are different from them are ignorant about the culture, beliefs, or practices of others. None of us is born with a preference for a particular race, gender, or religion. We develop our attitudes toward other people over time and through the influence of our families, friends, and the rest of society. Often, we learn from those around us to fear and disrespect things that we do not understand. If you are used to your own religion's rituals, the practices of another religion may seem strange or even wrong to you. However, the more we learn about people who are part of a different religion, race, class, or culture, the better we understand them and the better we are able to treat them in a tolerant manner.

Tolerance helps people around us by providing them with equal treatment. Many people would argue that it also benefits us as individuals. Life is more colorful when we have

U.S. President George W. Bush shows his respect for Chinese culture by wearing a traditional-style silk jacket while visiting Chinese President Jiang Zemin in Shanghai, China, in 2001.

friends and acquaintances from other cultures or classes who can enrich our lives with information and ideas to which we might not otherwise be exposed.

HUMAN RIGHTS

Another aspect of fairness and justice in action is human rights. According to the Universal Declaration of Human Rights, written in 1948 and adopted by the General Assembly of the United Nations, human rights refer to "recognition of the inherent dignity and of the equal and inalienable rights of all members of the human family. . . ." Those who advocate human rights work to bring freedom of speech and religion and freedom from fear and poverty to people all over the world. By promoting these rights and others, we help make the world a fairer place, where governments treat their people with justice, where all people have the same opportunities to succeed and enjoy their lives, and where people and nations live according to the rule of law. A major aspect of human rights involves promoting the rights of women, children, and minorities—people who have long suffered from unequal and unfair treatment.

ISSUES CONNECTED WITH FAIRNESS AND JUSTICE

Fairness Laws

Although U.S. society and government are based on the concept of equality and justice, according to founding documents such as the Declaration of Independence and the Constitution, it was not until the twentieth century that fairness was really enforced with any kind of authority or consistency. Even today, many people argue, the United States is not a fully equal society: African Americans, women, and other minority groups still suffer unequal treatment in the workplace and through practices such as racial profiling, wherein a person's race, class, gender, or culture is taken into consideration in

RACIAL PROFILING

Racial profiling occurs when a person is unfairly treated as a criminal suspect because he or she is of a certain race, gender, class, or culture. For example, imagine that a young African-American man is driving down the street in a town that is made up mainly of whites. A few blocks away, a burglary has just been committed, reportedly by a young black man. When a police officer sees the young African American driving past, she pulls him over and arrests him on suspicion of having committed the burglary, simply because he matches the description of the suspect in terms of race.

Since the terrorist attacks of September 11, 2001, racial profiling has also been used in an attempt to provide additional security. At airports and other security checkpoints, people who fit the stereotype of a terrorist (usually men of Middle Eastern descent) are often detained and interrogated as suspects.

Although racial profiling necessarily treats people of different backgrounds differently, its proponents argue that it is a helpful way to protect society and prevent or solve crimes. Others, however, argue that any type of discrimination—even discrimination for a worthwhile purpose, such as preventing terrorism—is wrong and has no place in a society that claims to treat its people with equality, justice, and fairness.

considering whether or not a person is likely to commit particular crimes.

In order to ensure a more equal and just society, the U.S. government has passed several laws that promote fairness. Perhaps the best known of these laws is the Civil Rights Act of 1964, which prohibits discrimination in public places on the basis of race. One part of this law, Title VII, also makes it illegal to sexually harass people, mainly in the workplace.

A second Civil Rights Act, passed in 1965, makes it unlawful to utilize literacy tests or other obstacles to prevent people from voting. (For many years, polling stations required voters to pass a literacy, or knowledge, test in order to vote. Although it was easy for most whites, even those with little education, to pass, it was more difficult for blacks, who did not receive the same educational opportunities.) Thanks to this law, all people now have a much better chance of exercising their constitutional right to vote.

THE EQUAL RIGHTS AMENDMENT

African Americans faced terrible discrimination for centuries, since the time when they were first brought to the United States as slaves. As a result of the civil rights movement, the Civil Rights Acts of 1964 and 1965 were passed, ensuring that African Americans would no longer suffer prejudice in public places or in voting. While African Americans were finally beginning to receive fair treatment, another group was also struggling for equality in U.S. society: women.

The feminist movement began in the 1960s, around the same time as the civil rights movement. Although women had won the right to vote with the ratification of the Nineteenth Amendment in 1920, they still faced discrimination, especially in the workplace, where women generally made (and, in some cases, still make) far less money for the same amount of work than their male counterparts.

As part of their push for equal rights, suffragists drafted the Equal Rights Amendment (ERA). Originally written in 1921 by suffrage leader Alice Paul, shortly after women gained the right to vote, the ERA stated: "Equality of Rights under the law shall not be denied or abridged by the United States or any state on account of sex." This draft amendment has been introduced in Congress every year since 1923, but to date, it has never received the number of votes necessary (38 states) to become part of the U.S. Constitution. Today, many people argue that the ERA is no longer needed, because women's rights are covered sufficiently by other laws, including Title IX of the Educational Amendments of 1972. Nonetheless, it is likely that women's rights leaders will continue to push for passage of the ERA until it finally becomes law.

The Educational Amendments of 1972 have a section called Title IX that prevents discrimination on the basis of sex. This law applies to all educational institutions and programs that receive any type of federal funding. It ensures that women have the same educational opportunities as men, which helps them achieve greater equality and success in the workplace after they have completed their education.

The 1990 Americans with Disabilities Act prohibits discrimination on the basis of physical or mental disabilities. It also requires schools that receive federal funds to provide programs for all students, including those with special needs. For many years, young people with disabilities were separated from their fellow students and restricted to "special needs" classes that were often far inferior to the classes in which students without disabilities were taught. Today, as often as possible, students with special needs are being integrated into regular classes, where they can receive the same educational opportunities as other students. Workplaces, too, are making an effort to attract employees who have disabilities that might have made it impossible for them to work in offices in the past. By erecting wheelchair-access ramps and utilizing special equipment, such as telephones that can be used by the hearing impaired, businesses are finally providing all people with the chance to work for a living.

Student Elections

Although elections for positions in student government in schools are supposed to be open to all students, many people argue that these elections are often unfair. In some schools, the people who run in (and win) student government elections are frequently the most popular kids in school, rather than those who would be most qualified to run the student government. For many years, people have argued that when student elections are nothing more than popularity contests, it is impossible for the student government to function in the way it is supposed to: creating a school environment where all students feel comfortable speaking their minds and trying to make changes, and where no one is subjected to discrimination or mocking because he or she is different.

Today's schools are beginning to realize that past practices have often been unfair, and they are actively seeking creative ways to bring fairness to student government. Some schools have begun to use lottery systems to elect student government members, which guarantees all students an equal chance of becoming school leaders. Others are running the school government by means of student committees whose members change on a regular basis, allowing more people to take part.

School Rules and Policies

Many schools today, both public and private, have strict policies that cover topics such as appropriate dress and academic honesty. School officials argue that certain kinds of clothing—such as T-shirts with profanity or obscene images on them or blouses that show a lot of skin—can be a distraction to kids who are trying to learn. On the other hand, the young people who want to wear these items argue that they have the right to dress however they like. Some people argue that school dress codes and other rules, such as the requirement that students rise and say the Pledge of Allegiance in the morning, discriminate against students whose culture or religion requires them to dress in a particular manner or whose beliefs do not include the idea of pledging loyalty to a nation or a flag.

Making sure that all students are treated equally while also creating a school environment that upholds the values of the community is a difficult task that often results in controversy. Many schools are forming committees that have both adult and student members in order to try to find

When it is difficult for school officials and students to agree on fair practices, the court system must sometimes get involved. In 1999, Aimee Scarduzio (*right*), a student at Wallace Middle School in Waterbury, Connecticut, and her mother, Sherry, challenged the strict rules of her school's dress code in court. The judge, however, said public school students do not have a constitutional right to wear baggy jeans that could possibly hide weapons.

compromises that will respect everyone's opinions and also ensure fair treatment.

Racism

Racism—discriminating against people on the basis of race or color—has existed for as long as there have been human beings of different races. The term *racism* refers to the belief that one race is better than another and that people of different races necessarily possess certain characteristics.

Because racism has been institutionalized in many cultures of the world, including that of the United States, it is very hard for people to push past it and treat one another with the fairness and justice to which all people are entitled.

Many people throughout history have fought hard to overcome racism and win fair treatment for all people. Perhaps

WHAT IS FAIR USE?

Today, with the large amount of written and broadcast materials in print, on television and radio, and on the Internet, the issue of fair use has become highly controversial. Fair use refers to the right to utilize someone else's work (such as a piece of writing) for your own purposes. When a person creates something original (such as a complete novel), he or she can apply for a copyright. A copyright protects the creator's right to reproduce, use, or authorize others to use his or her work for a specific period of time (in the United States, that period usually lasts until 70 years after the creator's death). But just how much of another person's work you can use without securing his or her permission is a difficult issue. It depends upon the type and length of the work and the reason you are using it (whether for personal use or to make a profit.) There are many guidelines and rules available online or through the U.S. Copyright Office, but the exact standards of what you can use are still being debated.

Music is one particularly controversial area in the fair use debate. In 2001, a Web site called Napster became embroiled in a legal fight. The purpose of Napster was to provide people with free music. Those who registered on the site could upload music and "share" songs with other users, who could then download the music for no cost. The music industry was outraged because artists were not earning royalties from this so-called file sharing. Several record companies sued Napster, which stopped providing free music in July 2001. Although it is still possible to download music from the Internet, according to the rules of fair use, people now must pay a fee to do so. This practice ensures justice for all concerned.

the best-known example is Martin Luther King Jr. (1929–1968), whose nonviolent efforts to oppose racism—including boycotts, marches, and sit-ins—helped spark the civil rights movement and won King the Nobel Peace Prize in 1964. Even today, more than 40 years after he was assassinated, King remains a symbol of the possibility that the United States may one day be a completely free and equal society.

Teen Rights

One of the most controversial arenas in which fairness and justice are involved today is the issue of teen rights. The question of whether young people are entitled to the same rights and privileges as adults has long divided society. The U.S. Supreme Court, which has ruled on several cases involving teen rights, has been inconsistent in its decisions involving the issue. For example, the court has allowed school newspapers to be censored by school or public officials, despite the First Amendment guarantee of the right to a free press, because it believes that schools have a role in teaching students what is good journalism. It has also allowed athletes to be randomly tested for drug use. Although a school has every right to prohibit its athletes from taking drugs if they wish to participate in school sports programs, some people argue that administering random drug tests to all athletes, whether drug use is suspected or not, invades students' privacy. In addition, the court has prohibited formal prayers or blessings at school events but has ruled that individual students have the right to pray in school. The debate over the extent to which teenagers enjoy rights equal to those of adults will likely go on for many years to come.

WHAT IS HONESTY?

2

Honesty is the first chapter in the book of wisdom.

—Thomas Jefferson (1743–1826),
third president of the United States

I t is very easy to define honesty: It simply means that you tell the truth; behave honorably; and do not lie, cheat, or steal. You are careful to remain true to the facts, avoiding bias or exaggeration, even if bending the truth would be to your advantage. An honest person is truthful not only to other people but also to him- or herself.

Being honest also means understanding that the truth is the foundation on which our society and everything in it—from business to education to art to family—are based. Without it, most people can never have peace of mind or achieve true success. As the old saying goes, "Honesty is the best policy." There are many different forms of honesty.

ACADEMIC HONESTY

Academic honesty means being honest in an educational setting. Someone who is academically honest does not commit plagiarism, which means copying someone else's work or using someone else's work without his or her permission. Plagiarism includes:

❋ Buying or copying someone else's work (such as a term paper) and passing it off as your own
❋ Copying from someone else's paper during a quiz or test
❋ Paying another person to do your school work

Other forms of academic dishonesty include doing someone else's work, changing your grades or academic record through forgery, stealing or ruining property that belongs to the school, lying about or exaggerating data to make the results from your work seem more believable, and cheating on a test or other assignment by using notes or other resources that you are not supposed to be using.

In order to prevent academic dishonesty, many schools have developed honor codes. These are statements that students sign or pledge to follow in which they promise not to cheat, plagiarize, or commit any other form of academic dishonesty. Students may also be required to turn in another student if they witness someone being dishonest in school. An honor code might say something like, "I pledge to pursue academic honesty as a student of this school. I understand that I am expected to do my own work and that working with someone else should be approved by the teacher. If I work with others or use portions of their work, I will acknowledge this in writing. I understand that it is my responsibility to report any form of academic dishonesty that I witness to the appropriate school authority." Often, students must sign this pledge whenever they take a test or turn in any assignment. Clearly, academic honesty is something that is taken very seriously in today's society.

INTEGRITY

People often used the words *honesty* and *integrity* interchangeably. Although they do have similar meanings, integrity is a broader term. Whereas honesty means telling the truth, integrity means being yourself and not putting on an act

TESTS OF HONESTY

There is an old saying, "Character is what you do when nobody is looking." It is easy to be honest when we are around people who are watching and judging our actions. If someone drops a $20 bill in a crowded store and other people see a person pick it up, that person is much more likely to give it back to the person who dropped it than she would be if no one had seen what happened. So, how often do people demonstrate good character when "nobody's looking"?

One study conducted by staff members of *Reader's Digest* magazine in 1997 set up an experiment in which more than a hundred wallets were left out in various places, where people would find them and assume that they were "lost" by their owners. Each wallet had $50 in cash in it, along with the name and address of the "owner." After the researchers put out the wallets, they sat back and waited to see how many would be returned, which would show how many people had the strength of character to do the right thing.

In the end, 56 percent of the wallets were returned. That meant that 44 percent—almost half—of the people who found the wallets decided just to take the money and ignore the fact that someone had lost his or her wallet. The researchers found, however, that in certain countries, people were more honest than in other countries. The most honest countries, according to the study, were Denmark and Norway. The people there returned a full 100 percent of the wallets. By contrast, in Hong Kong only 30 percent of the wallets were returned, and in Mexico, only 21 percent made it back to their "owners." Americans turned out to be in the middle when it comes to honesty—67 percent of the wallets in the United States were returned.

or pretending you are something you are not around others or even when you are by yourself. For example, people who have integrity wouldn't try to make others think they are wealthier than they really are or claim to have done something they haven't actually done to try to impress people.

Having integrity means that you remain true to the ideals that you value. You are reliable and consistent in your views, and people can count on you to do the things you promise to do. Integrity also means avoiding gossip or making fun of others, or pretending you know popular or famous people just to look cool.

SINCERITY

Sincerity means that you behave in an open and honest way, that you are genuine. You don't lie, exaggerate, or try to flatter people to get them to like you, and you are not a hypocrite. Put simply, to be sincere is to mean what you say and do.

On occasions, it can be difficult to be sincere, especially when you are around people you care about. Imagine that your best friend gets a new haircut that you think looks terrible. When she asks you how you like her new hairstyle, how do you respond? Technically, to be sincere, you would be compelled to tell her the truth, that you hate her haircut. But that would certainly hurt her feelings, since she likes you and trusts your opinion. The best way to behave in such a situation is to find something positive about the haircut (or outfit or whatever your friend is asking your opinion on) and focus on that when you respond. For example, you might say, "The bangs really bring out your eyes." This way, you are not lying, and at the same time, you are protecting your friend's feelings from being unnecessarily hurt.

SCIENTIFIC HONESTY

Honesty in science has become a hot issue over the last several decades, as new scientific advances are being made on a daily basis. Someone who is honest in the scientific arena is careful to be accurate in collecting and reporting data that result from research and experiments. He or she does not fake experiment results just to confirm a hypothesis or to look good.

Scientific honesty is extremely important. The public needs to be able to trust the results of scientific research and feel confident that the inventions, drugs, and other products that have been created are safe and effective. To try to make sure the scientific results that the public receives from scientists are correct, most technical journals that publish accounts of experiments and long-term studies are peer-reviewed. Having fellow scientists review and confirm the accuracy of experiments helps protect the public from dishonest researchers who are looking for a quick way to become rich and famous.

HONOR

Having honor means having a sense of fairness and always striving to do the right thing, no matter what the situation is. An honorable person can be relied on to be truthful in both words and actions. Someone who has honor will go out of his or her way to stand up for the truth, even when it would be easier just to keep silent. The honorable person doesn't let one person get blamed for something another did and doesn't let someone take credit for something he or she hasn't really done. As poet Adrienne Rich noted, "Lying is done with words and also with silence."

It is not always easy to know what the right thing to do is. But if you want to be an honorable person, you take the time to figure it out and you are willing to experience discomfort if necessary to do what is right.

Honor also includes another element: not taking what you do not deserve, either in terms of material goods or credit and intangible benefits. For example, if a cashier in a store accidentally gives you an extra five dollars in change, you will return it if you want to be an honorable person. Or, if you work with another student on a project and your teacher praises you for something the other person did, you make sure to give credit where it is due.

TRUSTWORTHINESS

Being trustworthy means that people can depend on you to do what you are supposed to do. Your parents can trust you to be home by curfew, your teachers can rely on you to be on time for class (and to show up for class, period), and your friends know that you will be there for them to talk to and will show up when you have agreed to go somewhere. This does not mean that you cannot ever be late if you want to be trustworthy. Everybody is late occasionally, and sometimes people even get so busy that they forget about social obligations, but trustworthy people will call if they are running late. However, a trustworthy person remembers his or her responsibilities and honors them as often as possible.

SPORTSMANSHIP

Sportsmanship means showing honesty and honor when you participate in athletic activities and other games. Someone who is a "good sport" behaves in a dignified way and treats others with respect, whether he or she wins or loses. Shaking hands with the other players after a game and telling someone that they made a good play, even when that play is to your disadvantage, are ways to exhibit sportsmanship. Demonstrating good sportsmanship also means being gracious in accepting the situation when an umpire or other official makes a bad call.

We typically learn sportsmanship from the adults around us—parents, coaches, teachers, as well as professional athletes. We become good sports when we learn that winning is not everything and that the way we play our chosen sport is just as important as being the best at it. In fact, winning should be only one out of many goals when we play sports. Other goals include developing our skills and getting better at the sport, as well as learning how to play by the rules and how to be a part of a team.

Too often in our society, good sportsmanship is ignored in favor of winning at all costs. Even professional athletes and teams have been known to cheat or bend the rules in order to excel. This dishonest behavior is also found among student athletes. In fact, when a 2006 survey by the Josephson Institute questioned more than 5,275 high school student

Being a "good sport" means getting along with people on your own team, as well as people who are your direct competition. Above, golfer Tiger Woods (*right*) laughs with competitor Rocco Mediate after winning the 108th U.S. Open in 2008. Woods won after a hard-fought playoff in which the two men were tied after 18 holes of golf, and then played a final "sudden death" hole to determine the winner.

athletes, results showed that those who play sports admit to cheating academically at a higher rate than those who do not play sports. This may be because many student athletes are required to maintain a certain grade point average in order to continue playing, because they may be more competitive by nature, or because it can be difficult for them to keep on getting good grades when they are spending so much time on the playing field. Whatever the reason, research shows that being dishonest in sports is linked to being dishonest in other aspects of life.

ISSUES CONNECTED WITH HONESTY

It is not always easy to be honest. Sometimes life presents us with situations that test our ability to remain truthful. Often, it seems as if things will work out better for us in the end if we choose to be dishonest. In fact, it can be a real struggle

HONESTY WITH A REFEREE

When Jana Benally was in fourth grade, her teacher asked her if she was chewing gum. Instead of telling the truth, she swallowed the gum and said that she hadn't been chewing any. Then, in fifth grade, Benally's class was assigned a big social studies project. To make the project go faster and to ensure that they all got good grades, Benally and her friends divided the assignment into smaller parts, on which each of them worked. Then they all copied from one another and turned in the completed project. When she collected the students' notebooks and went through them, the teacher noticed that Benally and her friends' work were exactly the same. She called Benally and the others into a conference with their parents to discuss the matter. Benally confessed to cheating and swore that she would never be dishonest again.

Benally's vow to be honest was tested a few years later, when she was a sophomore at San Juan High School and a star member of the volleyball team. During a state championship game, she returned a ball with a dramatic spike, which set up her team to win. However, Benally realized that when she had lunged to hit the ball, she had accidentally touched the net with her arm, which was against the rules. Although no one else had noticed, and she could have remained silent and allowed her team to use the incident to its advantage, she decided that she had to tell the truth. She stopped the referee and told him she had touched the net. The other team was awarded the point and went on to win the game.

Benally's teammates were angry, but they did not say anything to her after the game. Despite the fact that her actions had cost her team the game, Benally said she knew she had done the right thing.

to be honest in the face of temptations to lie, cheat, or steal. It can be difficult—actual, hard work—to be honest, while it is often easy to be dishonest. It takes time and energy to be honest, and this goes against what many people want in our modern society. People may feel that they deserve certain things—whether it is a house, a car, or a good relationship—and they want those things *now*. If it is easier to get them by lying, some people would rather do that than do the work of getting ahead the honest way.

It is also difficult to be honest when it seems like everybody else is being dishonest. It is easy to give in to the temptation to lie, cheat, or steal when people see these things going on all around them, and especially when people see others benefiting from their dishonesty. There are problems with being dishonest, however. When you tell a lie, you often have to keep telling additional lies to cover up the fact that you lied in the first place. And usually, lies do catch up with people in the end. Being dishonest can take a toll on friendships and other relationships. According to psychologist and researcher Dr. Lewis Andrews in his 1989 book *To Thine Own Self Be True*, there is evidence to suggest that dishonesty harms people, both psychologically and physically, because lying can put a lot of stress on their nervous systems. What are some of the everyday situations in which honesty may be tested? The following section examines some of the most common tests of honesty.

Cheating

Cheating means deceiving or misleading in order to achieve a better result, such as a better grade on a test or a win on the ball field. It is also considered cheating to use someone else's work or ideas without giving them credit.

There are many reasons why people choose to cheat. Some are determined to get good grades, perhaps to get into college or to be able to keep playing sports. Some are just lazy and do not want to put in the time and effort it takes to study and earn good grades honestly. Others may feel as if they are not smart enough to pass a test without cheating, so they cheat in order to avoid looking stupid.

People who cheat try to justify their behavior in different ways. Some say it is okay because everybody is doing it. Other people claim that the state and federal government have put standards in place for achievement that many cannot live up to without cheating. Still others see cheating as the easy way to get through school or through other experiences, and they see no need to do the work it would take to be honest.

New England Patriots coach Bill Belichick, shown with his team in 2007, became embroiled in a videotaping scandal that same year. Belichick was accused of cheating by having the New York Jets coaches' defensive signals videotaped. Punishment included a fine of 12 percent of his salary that year.

Despite widespread cheating, the vast majority of people understand that there is something valuable—namely, a real education and self-respect—that is gained by *not* cheating. Students interviewed for the pbs.kids.org Web site's "It's My Life" section state that cheating is not worth it because you are only cheating yourself and your own character. Eleven-year-old Capri posted her opinion on the site, saying, "You should never cheat. . . . You do not learn anything. I think it causes more trouble to yourself than the other person. Cheating will not solve the problem!"

Lying

Almost everyone can remember a time when he or she was faced with the temptation to tell a lie, even if it was just a small "white lie" or one that was intended to protect someone else's feelings. Still, the fact that people lie means that they are willing to be dishonest in certain situations.

In 2005, *Reader's Digest* magazine conducted an online poll about honesty, listing 16 dishonest acts, such as lying on a job application or resumé or sneaking into a movie without paying. A total of 1,985 readers responded. More than half admitted that they had committed between 9 and 16 of the listed acts, although only 4 percent admitted that they had committed *all* of the acts. Those who admitted to having been dishonest explained their behavior by saying that they had lied to "keep the peace," to protect the feelings of a loved one, or to preserve an intimate relationship. According to the survey, however, people seem to become more honest as they mature. One respondent explained, "I've noticed all my 'yes' answers were for when I was young. I'm older and wiser now, and believe in karma and the golden rule."

Fulfilling promises, holding on to friendships, and keeping a job or academic reputation intact are all common reasons why people lie. It is easy to give in to the temptation to lie, or simply to avoid telling the whole truth, when being honest could jeopardize our standing in the community or the way our friends and family look at us. Still, many people believe that honesty is a keystone of a fair and equal society. To that end, 97 percent of the young people interviewed for the 2006 Josephson Institute study said they agreed with the statement, "It's important to me that people trust me."

Stealing

Stealing means taking something that belongs to another person without having his or her permission. Taking anything—from a stick of gum to a yacht—is stealing. People can also steal ideas, such as someone's written work or project. In our modern society, where term papers and other works are easily available over the Internet, the theft of ideas is more common than ever.

There are many reasons why people steal. Some people—especially very young children, under the age of five or six—may not know any better. Some people who steal do not have a well-developed sense of self-control. Others may steal to bring things into their lives, such as designer clothing or favorite snack foods, that are missing because they can't afford or don't want to buy them. Some may steal to try to get attention from their parents or peers. Regardless of the underlying reason, people who steal are dishonest and do not recognize the importance of rules or laws.

People who steal things often don't realize the consequences of their actions—until they get caught. Thieves can be arrested and may have to serve time in jail or in a youth detention facility. Stealing is also dangerous because it can become a habit. Once taking other people's things becomes something a person is willing to do without remorse, it becomes easier to be dishonest in other ways.

It goes without saying that everyone would like to be wealthy or at least have anything they want. Yet, according to the 2006 Josephson Institute study, 89 percent of young people agreed with the statement, "Being a good person is

Personal gain is the biggest reason most people steal. In 2004, Edvard Munch's world famous painting, "The Scream," was stolen in a daytime raid by masked gunmen at the Munch Museum in Oslo, Norway. The thieves' intention was to sell the painting illegally. Police recovered the damaged painting in 2006.

more important than being rich." In other words, most of those studied agreed that choosing not to steal would make them good people.

3 SITUATIONS THAT TEST HONESTY AND FAIRNESS

It is hard to believe that a man is telling the truth when you know that you would lie if you were in his place.
—Henry Louis Mencken (1880–1956), American journalist

Every day, people are exposed to situations that require them to choose whether to be honest or fair. Although most people like to think of themselves as honest, the truth is that it can be hard to resist the temptation to lie, cheat, or steal, especially when the stakes are high, such as in sports or in school.

CHEATING IN SCHOOL

Academic honesty is one of the most commonly violated forms of honesty in today's society. Yet, people have been cheating to get ahead in school for generations. According to a research study done by Donald McCabe at Rutgers University in 2001, however, the amount of cheating by students has been increasing over the years, and the advent of the Internet age has made cheating even more common.

McCabe took a survey of 2,294 students who were in their junior year of high school. The students came from 25 different schools across the United States (14 public schools

HOW STUDENTS CHEAT: A STUDY

These are some of the results Donald McCabe compiled from his survey of high school students in their junior year.

TYPE OF CHEATING	PERCENTAGE REPORTING THIS BEHAVIOR
Copied from another on test	63%
Used crib notes on test	39%
Got questions/answers from someone who had already taken a test	77%
Helped someone cheat on test	60%
Copied almost word for word and submitted the work	34%
Turned in work copied from someone else	68%
Turned in work done by parents	20%
Worked on assignment when told not to	76%
Copied a few sentences without citing	60%
Let someone copy homework	86%
Turned in paper obtained online	16%
Copied sentences from a Web site without footnoting	52%

and 11 private schools.) He asked them questions about their past and current behavior in regard to cheating, such as whether they had ever used crib (cheat) notes while taking a test, whether they had ever copied someone's work or let someone else copy theirs, and whether they had used a term paper or other piece of writing that they found on the Internet without giving the original author credit. More than half (and often more) of the students admitted to having committed most of the violations.

McCabe's results represented an increase in the rate of cheating that had been reported in previous studies, such as a 1989 study done by Louis Harris and sponsored by the Girl Scouts of the USA. This study found that two-thirds of the high school students interviewed said they would cheat to pass an important exam. These results, like those in the Rutgers study, also showed that cheating has become more common over the years.

Similarly, this trend has been confirmed by studies done by Fred Schab at the University of Georgia in 1969, 1979, and 1989. Schab found that the number of students who admitted to using crib notes on a test doubled between 1969 and 1989, from 34 percent to 68 percent. The numbers of those who let other students copy their work leaped from 58 percent in 1969 to an astounding 98 percent in 1989. These alarming statistics demonstrate how important it is for students to learn about good character early, so they can help make society more fair and honest, rather than become part of the problem.

Why is cheating so prevalent in schools today, and why does it become more common with each passing year? For one thing, parents are putting more pressure than ever on their children to do well in school and to get into college. In addition, the curriculum is getting more difficult in most schools over time. Some students feel like they have to cheat just to pass. This attitude is especially the case among high-achieving students, whose schoolwork is more difficult and who feel pressured to keep their grades up. As one advanced

CHEATERS: THE STORY OF STEINMETZ HIGH SCHOOL

The 2000 movie *Cheaters,* starring actor Jeff Daniels, told the true story of Steinmetz High School in Chicago. In 1995, the high school's team for the Illinois Academic Decathlon, led by English teacher Jerry Plecki, cheated by studying from a copy of the test that one of the team members had stolen. A student from the school also posed as a judge at the competition to help Steinmetz's team perform better than they would have done otherwise.

Because the Steinmetz team's scores in the contest were so high, the judges became suspicious that something was wrong. An investigation into the matter exposed the fact that the team had cheated. The Steinmetz team was stripped of its win in the decathlon, and teacher Jerry Plecki was forced to leave his position at the school. Even though more than a decade has passed since the incident took place, some people feel that Steinmetz High is still trying to live down the negative image the cheating gave to the school.

placement (AP) calculus student who was quoted in the Winter 2001 issue of *American Educator* explained: "I'm in there with some of the smartest people in school. . . . They are, like, always ready to cheat. . . . [The teacher] leaves most of the teaching up to the students and he'll throw, like, a chapter out there. . . . You gotta learn this. . . . It just drives people to cheat."

Other students claim that they cheat because they know they will not get caught. Some 26 percent of the students in the Rutgers study said that their teachers look the other way because they do not feel like going through all the trouble it would take to report the cheating and have the school investigate it.

The Internet has also played a major role in the increase in cheating over the past several years. Many students copy written work directly from the Internet or even buy term papers to use in school. Often, the students who use online sources do not even realize that what they are doing is wrong. According to McCabe, many high school students think any information found on the Internet is considered public knowledge and, therefore, does not have to be footnoted, even if it is used word for word.

To try to combat cheating that involves the Internet, several sites have been developed in recent years to provide educators with tools to scan their students' work for plagiarism. Sites such as Turnitin.com and IntegriGuard allow teachers to put students' work into a search engine that checks whether any of the information in the work has been copied from any source available on the Internet. Although such sites are great assets in curtailing online cheating, many students continue to use Web sites in inappropriate ways because they know that their teachers are not Internet-savvy enough to use the anti-plagiarism sites.

Another step that is often taken to prevent cheating is the adoption of an honor code. As previously noted, an honor code requires students to pledge not to cheat and, often, to promise to turn in anyone they witness cheating. Although many schools believe honor codes work, some argue that they turn students against one another and force many to lie about cheating—making an already bad problem even worse. Although following an honor code can be difficult, doing so will gain the respect of other students—especially those who do not cheat. By not cheating yourself and by doing the right thing and turning in people who do cheat, you make school fairer for everyone and ensure that everybody's grades are accurate.

LYING IN SCHOOL AND BUSINESS

Some people may lie to protect themselves when they make a mistake at work or to avoid hurting someone else's feelings. Even people who are generally honest may tell "white lies" to cover up their real feelings if telling the truth might cause problems in a relationship with a loved one.

Teenagers especially tend to lie to their parents. A 2001 article by David Knox on the Web site BNET (Business Network) presented the results of a study that surveyed 281 undergraduate college students about how much they had lied during high school. Knox found that 85 percent of the students admitted that they had lied at least once to their parents about where they were when they went out during their high school years. The study also found that the teens lied frequently about topics such as whom they were with, their sexual behavior, and whether or not they drank alcohol. In fact, almost all the things teens lied to their parents about were important issues, such as drug and alcohol abuse. And, as the data shows, the students were quite good at deceiving their parents. Only 5 percent said that they were often caught in lies. Interestingly, despite the fact that they admitted to lying, the vast majority—85 percent—of the students surveyed said that they considered themselves basically honest people. This may be attributed to the fact that 74.7 percent of the students said that they lie less now that they are a little bit older.

There are many other situations that might lead someone to lie. Business is one arena where lying is all too common. According to a 1989 study performed by the international public relations firm Pinnacle Group, 59 percent of the high school students surveyed said that they would willingly take part in an illegal business deal worth $10 million, even if it meant that they would face six months of criminal probation. Fifty percent said they would lie on insurance claims, and 66 percent would lie if it would help them achieve a business goal. Similarly, a poll conducted by Shearson-Lehman in 1992 questioned people between the ages of 18 and 29, and found that 39 percent believed that deceit was a useful way to get ahead in business. Still, researchers point out that to earn respect in business—both from yourself and from others—honesty is of the utmost importance. Few people would make a business deal with someone who is known to be a liar or cheater.

GOSSIP

What is the difference between talk and gossip? Can you talk about someone and not be gossiping? The answer is yes. Regular conversation means sharing your thoughts and ideas with other people. Gossip is sharing information with others that should be kept private or that you are not sure is accurate. Sometimes it can be difficult to determine whether it is right to talk about something you have heard or witnessed. Imagine that a friend told you his parents were getting a divorce, but he asked you to keep the information to yourself. You try to keep your friend's secret, but later, when you are hanging out with some other friends, the conversation lags and you think about telling the secret to have something to talk about. To do so would be gossiping—and you would also be betraying your friend's trust.

Sometimes you might find yourself on the receiving end of gossip. A friend might tell you a story about someone you both know. Before you take the information and repeat it, you need to remember that you did not get the story first-hand from the person involved: It is only gossip, and it may not be entirely—or even remotely—true. In fact, you should do your best to avoid even listening to gossip in the first place. Remember that if someone is telling you secrets about someone else, it is very possible that he or she is telling *your* secrets to other people.

DISHONESTY IN SPORTS

The temptation to cheat in order to win a game or to perform better in sports has existed as long as sports themselves have been around. A 2002 Josephson Institute study showed that high school students who play sports tend to cheat at a higher rate than those who are not athletes. Today, there are sophisticated ways to cheat that go beyond bribing officials or getting an unfair head start in a race. Modern science has allowed athletes to ingest drugs and even substances that mimic chemicals found in the body to help them run faster, play longer, be stronger, or get more hits in baseball. This form of cheating in sports is known as doping. Over the past several years, many athletes have been exposed for using illegal substances to improve their game.

Mark McGwire was one of professional baseball's leading hitters. He broke the record for the most home runs in a season in 1998. Yet, since his retirement from the game, it has come to light that he—and many of his fellow baseball

THE MITCHELL REPORT ON DOPING IN SPORTS

On December 13, 2007, former senator George Mitchell released a 409-page report that summed up the results of his 20-month-long investigation into the use of steroids and other illegal substances by Major League Baseball players. The report named 89 ballplayers who were found to have used illegal substances, including human growth hormone.

Mitchell's investigation relied mainly on information provided by two witnesses: former New York Mets clubhouse worker Kirk Radomski and personal trainer for the New York Yankees Brian McNamee. Based on interviews with these men, Mitchell determined that many leading players, including famed pitcher Roger Clemens, had been injected with steroids that led to dramatic improvements in their playing ability.

The report recommended that Major League Baseball improve the tests it uses to look for illegal substances in its players, and should go beyond the urine tests that are currently utilized. It also said that players should be better educated about the health dangers of steroids and other substances. Congress is continuing to look into charges of doping in baseball and other sports.

Dishonesty in sports includes those who take illegal substances in order to improve performance. Major League Baseball (MLB) player Mark McGwire used steroids and other performance-enhancing drugs, which reportedly helped him break the record in 1998 for the most home runs in a season. Above, McGwire is sworn in as players Sammy Sosa (*left*) and Rafael Palmeiro (*right*) look on during a 2005 federal government hearing into MLB's efforts to end steroid use among its players.

players—may have taken steroids or other illegal substances, such as human growth hormone, in order to build muscle and become better athletes. Jose Canseco, another athlete who admitted to doping, said that steroids were "as prevalent in . . . the late 1980s and 1990s as a cup of coffee."

The offenders were not just baseball players. Although he was eventually exonerated, record-breaking bicyclist Lance Armstrong was accused of doping through the use of a hormone called erythropoietin (EPO). Another cyclist, Floyd Landis, lost his title as the winner of the 2006 Tour de France when his illegal doping was exposed.

Since these stories about cheating athletes have come to light, professional sports organizations have been working hard to institute drug testing and other means of making sure that competition is fair and that no one has an illegal advantage. Many professional athletes are also speaking out to encourage future generations to avoid doping and other forms of cheating in order to preserve the integrity of sports.

One reason it has taken so long for sports doping to be noticed is that the tests for the substances being used are only now beginning to identify all of the products athletes can use to help their performance. And, even though athletes know they are risking their lives—doping products can cause long-term damage to the body and even sudden death due to heart failure—as well as their reputations, it can be hard for athletes to resist the temptation to improve their game by dramatic measures.

Doping is not just dangerous for the people who do it; it is bad for sports. Because it artificially improves players' performance, it prevents games from truly being fair, and it is a basic assumption that when we watch sports competitions, we are watching a fair contest. When someone wins because he or she has cheated by doping, the victory is meaningless and often less exciting.

FAIRNESS IN HISTORY

Fairness is what justice really is.

—*Potter Stewart (1915–1985), U.S. Supreme Court justice*

Even though most people like to think that they are fair-minded and that they would do their best to treat others with fairness and tolerance, history demonstrates that, a good deal of the time, human beings are anything but fair. Here, we examine some of the many instances throughout history where people have been treated unfairly and the ways in which they fought for equal treatment.

THE AFRICAN-AMERICAN STRUGGLE FOR EQUALITY

Slavery has existed for as long as humans have been recording their history, and probably longer. When Europeans first began to explore Africa in the 1400s, they began to buy and sometimes steal black Africans, whom they put to work as slaves. As European settlers sailed to America and started colonies in places such as Jamestown, Virginia, they brought the slave trade with them. It would go on in America for centuries, ending only in 1865 with the ratification of the Thirteenth Amendment, which prohibits slavery.

Black Africans did not just accept their fate and go willingly with the Europeans to become slaves. The Europeans

Throughout history, people have been treated without regard to human rights, and the slave trade is a prime example. This 1835 illustration shows slaves being shackled on a slave ship.

overpowered them with guns and sophisticated weapons that could kill those who tried to resist. Over time, some Africans became involved in the slave trade, raiding and kidnapping members of other communities and selling these captives to the Europeans. Slavery became an institution, a way of life that was difficult to change. In fact, as the United States won its independence and began to grow, the Southern states, which grew cash crops such as cotton and tobacco, came to depend on slave labor for their economic survival.

However, not everyone in the United States agreed that slave labor was a good thing. Even some of those who owned slaves themselves—including many of the Founding Fathers—hoped to find a way to free the blacks from the system that enslaved them. The third U.S. president, Thomas Jefferson, and his successor, James Madison, both became part of the American Colonization Society (ACS), a group formed in 1817 to promote the dismantling of the slave system and the transport of the freed slaves back to Africa. Although the members of the ACS believed slaves were being treated unfairly, they still were not willing to treat them with complete fairness. Rather than allowing them to become part of U.S. society, they believed it would be better for the slaves to leave the United States entirely. In 1822, the ACS set up a new colony, called Liberia, on the western coast of Africa. In 1847, it officially became a nation, and thousands of former slaves emigrated there from the United States.

The problem of slavery proved to be too big for the ACS to overcome. In many places in the South, the population of slaves was almost as large as that of whites. It would be impossible to send all of these people to Africa. In addition, by the 1800s, a large portion of the slaves had been born in the United States and no longer felt they had any direct ties to Africa. If slavery were to be abolished, the slaves would have to be accommodated in the United States.

Yet, not everyone wanted that to happen. Slavery was a way of life in the South, and Southerners fiercely defended what was sometimes called "the peculiar institution." As the United States expanded its territory to the west, slaves moved west, too. It became confusing and contentious for the U.S. Congress to figure out how to represent states with and without slaves. By 1861, the non-slaveholding North and the slave-owning South could no longer agree on how the American government should be run, and the Civil War began. The U.S. president at the time, Abraham Lincoln, is well known for the Emancipation Proclamation he issued in 1863, which freed the slaves in the states of the rebellious South. Contrary to popular belief, Lincoln did not free the slaves in any of the states that had remained loyal to the Union. It would take the North's victory in the Civil War to formally end slavery in 1865

SEPARATE BUT EQUAL: JUSTICE JOHN HARLAN AND THE CASE OF *PLESSY V. FERGUSON*

In 1896, the U.S. Supreme Court decided the case of *Plessy v. Ferguson*, which upheld a Louisiana law that forced blacks to ride in separate railroad cars from whites—a formal establishment of the "separate but equal" system created by the South's Jim Crow laws in the post–Civil War era. The court approved the law by a vote of 7 to 1 (one justice did not take part in the decision.) The lone dissenting justice was John Marshall Harlan. He wrote in his dissenting opinion: "In the eye of the law, there is in this country no superior, dominant, ruling class of citizens. There is no caste here. Our constitution is color blind, and neither knows nor tolerates classes among citizens."

Harlan's dissent was a surprising viewpoint, especially since it was coming from a man who had been born in Kentucky to a slaveholding family and had owned slaves himself once he became an adult. During the Civil War, Harlan supported the preservation of the Union, but at the same time, he believed that the federal government should not get involved in the question of slavery. He

Though he was once a slave owner who believed the government should not be involved in the issue of slavery, Justice John Marshall Harlan (*pictured above in 1907*) eventually joined the Republican Party and ruled against slavery and for the rights of blacks.

(continues)

(continued)

believed the states had the right to decide for themselves whether or not they would permit slavery within their borders. He said that U.S. government intervention in overturning slavery with the Thirteenth Amendment was "a flagrant invasion of the right of self-government which deprived the states of the right to make their own policies." He said that he would oppose the freeing of the slaves by the federal government even "if there were not a dozen slaves in Kentucky."

Just two years after making this statement, however, in 1867, Harlan made a sudden and dramatic reversal. He became a Republican and began to support the rights of black Americans. In 1871, he wrote, "I have lived long enough to feel and declare that . . . the most perfect despotism [governmental system in which the ruler has unlimited power] that ever existed on this earth was the institution of American slavery."

Harlan was aware of the contradiction between his earlier position and his new view after joining the Republican Party. However, he said, "Let it be said that I am right rather than consistent." Harlan's bold dissent in *Plessy v. Ferguson* paved the way for future justices to support the civil rights of African Americans.

with the ratification of the Thirteenth Amendment to the Constitution, which prohibited slavery in the United States.

Even after they were freed from slavery, blacks in America were not treated with fairness. In the post–Civil War years, the South passed laws, known as Jim Crow laws, that created separate public facilities, such as restrooms and water fountains, for blacks and whites. Restaurants, theaters, and even schools were divided by race. Supposedly, these public facilities were "separate but equal," but in reality, the facilities used by blacks were extremely inferior.

Through the late 1800s and the early twentieth century, blacks and sympathetic whites fought to have the Jim Crow laws overturned and for blacks and whites to receive equal treatment. In the 1950s and 1960s, the civil rights movement, led by black activists such as Martin Luther King Jr., began. Protesters demonstrated against separate but equal facilities and laws that prevented blacks from voting despite the fact that the Constitution guaranteed equal rights for all races. Gradually, through the passage of laws such as the 1964 Civil Rights Act, American society became fairer to all people, including blacks and other minorities. Although some people argue that, even today, black people are not treated with complete equality, the United States has come a very long way since the days of the slave trade.

Under Jim Crow laws, blacks and whites had "separate but equal" facilities. Above, a black boy drinks from a "colored" fountain in Halifax, North Carolina, in 1938.

EQUAL EDUCATION

For most of U.S. history, the public education system has been one of the least fair institutions in the country. Although most states required white children to attend school for at least a portion of the year, they were generally separated from black children and the children of other minorities, some of whom received little or no education at all. Not until the twentieth century and the start of the civil rights movement did the U.S. government finally start to make education equal for all children.

Desegregated education for black students did not happen easily. Above, Elizabeth Eckford walks past angry parents and students after being turned away by the Arkansas National Guard when she tried to enter Little Rock High School. It wasn't until days later that a federal judge had police escort Eckford and eight other black students into the previously all-white school.

THE FIGHT FOR PASSAGE
OF THE FIFTEENTH AMENDMENT

After the Civil War, the Thirteenth Amendment to the Constitution formally abolished slavery in 1865. The Fourteenth Amendment, ratified in 1868, promised that all Americans were entitled to due process of the law. Despite these amendments, however, the African Americans who had been freed from slavery after the war were not being granted the right to vote or other equal rights, especially in the South. To remedy this, Congress passed the Fifteenth Amendment in February 1869. It said that the states could not deny citizens the right to vote on the basis of race, color, or the fact that they had once been slaves. Still, getting the states to ratify the amendment and make it law took some work.

African-American activists and Republicans were the most outspoken supporters of the amendment. They were joined by many women who were members of the suffrage movement that was struggling to win the right to vote for women. These women hoped to get the amendment to include women, thereby giving women the right to vote. Even after it became clear that only men would be covered, some suffragists continued to fight to ratify the amendment, believing that if they helped black men win the vote now, those same men would then help women win the right to vote later.

Congress solved the problem of getting the Southern states to ratify the Fifteenth Amendment by forcing them to accept it if they wished to become part of the Union again, after having seceded during the Civil War. In March 1870, the Fifteenth Amendment officially became part of the U.S. Constitution, and blacks were guaranteed the right to vote. However, in many places, this right was only a theory. In reality, poll taxes, literacy tests, and grandfather clauses (which said that a person was not allowed to vote if his grandfather had not been permitted to vote) prevented many blacks from voting. The Ku Klux Klan, a white-supremist organization, also used violence to keep blacks from voting.

(continues)

(continued)

These barriers to the vote existed until the middle of the twentieth century in some areas.

Women were even more disappointed in their quest for the right to vote. Despite their help in winning ratification of the Fifteenth Amendment, African-American men did not take part in the women's suffrage movement as the suffragists had hoped. Although leading suffragists tried to argue that the Fifteenth Amendment should apply to women as well as men, they were ignored. To try to promote their position, several women tried to vote in the 1868 election. Rather than being granted equal treatment, they were arrested. Women would not win the right to vote until the ratification of the Nineteenth Amendment in 1920.

During the Jim Crow era, black and white children attended separate schools, while many Native American children were forced to attend special schools where they were prevented from speaking their tribal languages and performing their cultural rituals. In 1954, the U.S. Supreme Court decided the case of *Brown v. Board of Education of Topeka, Kansas.* This case had originally been started by the parents of a young African-American girl named Linda Brown, who, because of the existence of "separate but equal" schools in her town, had to walk a mile, past white schools that were closer to her home, in order to reach the all-black school she attended. The Supreme Court ruled that schools could no longer be legally segregated by race, noting, "Segregation of white and colored children in public schools has a detrimental effect upon the colored children. . . . A sense of inferiority affects the motivation of a child to learn." As the court put it, "separate educational facilities are inherently unequal."

The states, particularly those of the South, did not immediately put the ruling into effect. Many thought they could get away with ignoring the order to integrate and continue to treat blacks and other minorities unfairly when it came to education. By 1957, however, the national spotlight was shining on the city of Little Rock, Arkansas, where a group of African-American students was preparing to enter the previously all-white Central High School. In an attempt to stop the process of integration, Arkansas governor Orval Faubus called out the state's National Guard to block the students from entering the school. A few tense days passed, but finally, a federal judge forced the National Guard to withdraw, and on Monday, September 23, police escorted nine African Americans into Central High. After centuries of unequal treatment, blacks were finally beginning to receive an unsegregated, fairer education.

Colleges, too, were desegregated after the *Brown* decision. In 1962, James Meredith became the first African-American student to attend the University of Mississippi. Although his entrance to the school in October sparked a riot in which two people were killed, his acceptance and attendance at "Ole Miss," as the university is called, paved the way for equal treatment of African Americans in higher education.

THE TREATMENT OF NATIVE AMERICANS

Like the Africans, Native Americans found themselves facing unfair treatment after they first encountered European colonists in the sixteenth century and beyond. From the time white people began to settle in America, they forced the natives off their traditional lands, signed treaties of peace and protection that they quickly violated or ignored, or captured and enslaved the natives. The superiority of European weapons, along with the diseases to which Native Americans had no immunity, killed Native Americans in huge numbers and enabled the Europeans to subdue them.

Another reason the Native Americans were vulnerable to unfair treatment was because most could not read or write. Although some tribes did have their own languages, most had no written language. A Cherokee warrior named

Sequoyah set out to overcome his people's illiteracy and make it easier for them to communicate with one another and thereby better defend themselves against the encroachment of white settlers.

The Cherokee warrior Sequoyah fought against the unfair treatment of Native Americans by introducing a system of writing to his people in 1821. Here, in an image drawn around 1836, Sequoyah is shown holding a tablet with the Cherokee alphabet he created.

Having served under General Andrew Jackson during the War of 1812, Sequoyah had seen how illiteracy limited the Native Americans' ability to communicate. The illiterate Cherokee soldiers could not write letters to loved ones at home or read orders from their military leaders. After the war, Sequoyah returned home and began to work on a syllabary—essentially an alphabet of symbols—that would form the basis of the Cherokee written language. He introduced his system of writing to his people in 1821. In just a few months, thousands of Cherokee learned the system and became able to read and write.

Unfortunately, the Cherokee people's ability to use Sequoyah's syllabary did not stop whites from treating them unfairly. In fact, it was during the mid-1800s, the same time when Sequoyah was teaching the Cherokee to read and write, that the U.S. government began its systematic removal of the Native Americans from the East, where whites were settling in large numbers, across the Mississippi River to the West, to reservations set aside for the natives to live on. By 1840, all of the eastern tribes had been moved west to the Indian Territory (present-day Oklahoma). The forced removals, including the difficult journey along what became known as the Trail of Tears, had tragic effects on the Native Americans. Many did not survive the journey, while a big proportion of those who did had trouble adjusting to the very different environment. When the first Europeans came to America, there were approximately 10 million Native Americans living there. Three hundred years later, 90 percent of the natives had been killed off by disease, hunger, or warfare.

Along with other minorities, including African Americans and women, Native Americans began to demand equal rights during the early and mid-1900s and to protest the unfair treatment that the various tribes had endured for centuries. In 1968, the American Indian Movement (AIM) was founded by Dennis Banks, Clyde Bellecourt, and other Native American activists. Russell Means joined soon after and quickly became one of its most prominent leaders. AIM pressed the U.S. government to honor the treaties it had made and broken with the Native Americans in the past and to make life on the Indian reservations more tolerable. Over the years, many of the natives who were forced onto reservations found themselves living in poverty, without a decent education, and often in hunger. AIM sought to turn around the lives of Native Americans and to gain respect for their way of life,

American Indian Movement leaders Dennis Banks (*left*) and Russell Means (*right*) give a press conference in 1973 to demand that the U.S. government increase financial aid to the town of Wounded Knee, South Dakota.

and restore the many native traditions that had been lost (or forcefully eliminated by the government) over the years.

Although Native Americans today—especially those living on the reservations—still face problems and unequal education and business opportunities, the work of AIM and other activist groups has forced the U.S. government to acknowledge that the way natives were treated in the past was wrong and to look for ways to make Native American life better. With the establishment of casinos and other tourist attractions that have been set up on reservations and provide jobs for many Native Americans, many native people today are beginning to see a dramatic improvement in their lives as people are more respectful and show an interest in learning about the Native American way of life.

TAXATION WITHOUT REPRESENTATION

Minorities are not the only ones who have been treated unfairly in the past. Even the English colonists who settled America faced unfair treatment at the hands of England. England established the American colonies with an eye to making money from the many resources that the New World had to offer. In return for the American trade, England promised to protect the colonists from settlers of other national origins, such as the French, and from the Native Americans who often tried to prevent the whites from taking over their lands.

Over time, however, the colonists began to believe that England was not treating them fairly. That is, they believed that they were being treated differently from their fellow English citizens who still lived in the mother country. As Englishmen, the colonists believed they were entitled to have representatives in Parliament (the English legislature) to promote their interests. After all, they paid taxes to England, and all the other English people who paid taxes had representation in the legislature. Many educated colonists, such as Samuel Adams, Thomas Paine, and George Washington, who would later become the first U.S. president, began to protest the policy of "taxation without representation." In fact, their anger at the unfair way England was treating the colonies eventually led to an outright rebellion, which grew to become the American Revolution in which the colonists won their independence from England and started a government of their own. Their new government guaranteed the people who paid taxes (at the time, mainly white, land-owning males) representation in Congress. Since the American Revolution, giving the people adequate representation has become a cornerstone of the U.S. government.

CHILD LABOR

Today in the United States, children and young adults are expected to attend school, rather than work at full-time jobs. People consider getting a good education and having plenty of time to rest and play a fair life for children. This has not always been the case.

It was not until the late nineteenth and early twentieth centuries that child labor was examined and determined to be wrong. In fact, the number of child laborers in America peaked in the early decades of the twentieth century. In 1900, the U.S. Census showed that about 2 million children were working in factories and mills, as well as other jobs. Considering how poor most people were all over the world during the nineteenth century and that the Industrial Revolution forced people off farms and into factories to earn a living, it is not surprising that children had to work in order to help their families survive. However, by the mid-nineteenth century, some people began to believe that it was wrong to put young children into dangerous jobs and force them to work long hours that damaged their health and prevented them from getting an adequate education.

In 1832, the New England Association of Farmers, Mechanics, and Other Workingmen said that child labor was wrong, stating, "Children should not be allowed to labor in the factories from morning till night, without any time for healthy

The concept of letting children have a fair childhood of play and rest did not always exist. In the early part of the twentieth century, child labor was prevalent. Above, a group of oyster shuckers works in a canning factory in Louisiana in 1911. The group—young and old—worked each day from 3:30 A.M. to 5 P.M.

recreation and mental culture." Four years later, the state of Massachusetts passed the first child labor law, requiring children under the age of 15 to attend school for at least three months each year.

One of the best-known opponents of child labor in the nineteenth century was the famous British novelist Charles Dickens. In his 1838 novel *Oliver Twist*, Dickens described the dangerous chimney-sweep business, in which many boys toiled. Drawing on his own experience as a child laborer who worked in a factory at the age of 12, Dickens wrote the novel, *David Copperfield*. In it, he noted, "I know enough of the world now to have lost the capacity of being much surprised by anything; but it is a matter of some surprise to me, even now, that I can have been so easily thrown away at such an age."

American photographer Lewis Hine also contributed to the fight to against child labor. His dramatic photos of labor conditions in the United States drew public attention to the horrors of child labor and helped bring about laws that limited the number of hours and days children were permitted to work.

This photograph, taken by Lewis Hine, shows two young girls who worked as spinners in a cotton mill. Photographs like these helped expose the horrible conditions and unfairness of child labor, and led to laws that limited the number of hours each day that a child could work.

In 1904, the National Child Labor Committee was founded and began an aggressive campaign to reform child labor laws. In 1916, the Keating-Owen Child Labor Act—the first federal child labor law—was passed. It used Congress's power to regulate interstate commerce to control child labor. It said that goods could not be moved across state lines if child labor had been used to create them. By 1938, minimum ages and maximum working hours for children had been set. Since then, both Congress and the states have continued to monitor children's working conditions to make sure that all U.S. children have a fair chance to attend school and get enough rest and recreation to lead healthy lives.

GIVING ALL LABORERS FAIR TREATMENT

Although guilds or trade unions—groups of workers who devote themselves to protecting the interests of their members—have existed since the Middle Ages, it was not until the nineteenth and twentieth centuries that the labor union became a powerful voice in favor of the fair treatment of workers by business owners and managers. Before the Industrial Revolution, people tended to work either for themselves on farms or as artisans who were part of guilds. With the advent of machinery that took over many jobs humans had done before, many people needed to work in factories and other industries to make a living. Because working-class people were so dependent on their jobs for survival, factory owners were able to force them to work almost unlimited hours and virtually every day without a break and under dangerous conditions in hot, unventilated buildings.

By the mid-nineteenth century, workers began to organize in order to protest the bad treatment by their employers. In 1866, the National Labor Union pushed Congress to make an eight-hour workday standard. Although this legislation passed, it was repealed in 1873, when the country went into a depression. Workers were not deterred, however. They established the Knights of Labor in 1869 to try to protect the rights of both skilled and unskilled workers. Then, in 1886, Samuel Gompers founded the American Federation of Labor (AFL). According to a statement the union issued, its purpose was "To protect the skilled labor of America from being reduced to beggary and to sustain the standard of American workmanship and skill."

When railroad workers at the Pullman plant in Chicago went on strike in 1894, they were led by American socialist Eugene V. Debs. Although the strike ultimately failed because

LECH WALESA AND THE SOLIDARITY MOVEMENT

One of the most successful labor movements of the twentieth century was the Solidarity movement that took place in Poland. Led by a former mechanic and shipyard worker named Lech Walesa, the movement fought for the rights of workers during the 1970s and 1980s.

Under the Communist government that led Poland at the time, workers were not allowed to strike or to form unions that were not part of the official Communist system. Starting in 1978, Walesa helped form non-Communist unions and led them in demonstrations aimed at improving conditions for workers. Although he was frequently arrested, Walesa became known all over the world for speaking out on behalf of workers. He won support from world leaders, including Pope John Paul II, who invited Walesa to visit the Vatican in 1981. That same year, the Polish government suspended the Solidarity movement and put Walesa under house arrest in the country.

Public support for Walesa continued, however, and in 1983, he was awarded the Nobel Peace Prize. Although the Polish government denounced the idea of giving the Nobel Prize to Walesa, he continued to gain so much power that the government was eventually forced to negotiate with him and his fellow labor leaders. The government finally the workers had no money or other means to feed their families and had to give up and return to work, Debs became a major union leader who spent the rest of his life trying to improve conditions for U.S. laborers.

Another famous labor union leader was A. Philip Randolph. Randolph was unique in that he fought not only for the fair treatment of workers but also for the equal treatment of African-American workers. He organized a union called the Brotherhood of Sleeping Car Porters (BSCP) and also served on the executive council of the AFL after it merged with

Lech Walesa speaks to the striking workers he fought for after negotiating a preliminary contract between the workers and the Polish government in 1980.

agreed to hold parliamentary elections, which led to the overturn of the Communist government. In 1990, Walesa was elected president of the Republic of Poland. He remains one of the best-known labor leaders of all time.

Eugene Victor Debs led a railroad workers' strike in Chicago in 1894, and spent the rest of his life fighting for U.S. laborers' rights. Debs had been sentenced to ten years in prison for criticizing the Espionage Act during a speech in Ohio in 1918, but was pardoned by President Warren G. Harding in 1921. Above, he is shown after his release from a federal prison.

another union called the Congress of Industrial Organizations to form the AFL-CIO.

The hard work of these leaders and many others during the early and mid-twentieth century paid off. Congress passed laws to ensure that workers received a minimum wage and could only be required to work eight hours a day.

EQUAL TREATMENT FOR FARMERS

The United States was originally founded as a nation based on farming. Over time, however, as cities grew and industries sprang up, farming became less common, but no less important, since Americans still depended on the farmers to provide them with food, whether they lived in rural or urban areas. By 2003, only 1 percent of people in the United States still lived on farms.

Despite the fact that there are fewer farmers today than ever, farms are still capable of producing a great deal more food than is necessary to feed the people of the United States and to export food to other countries. When too many crops are put up for sale on the free market, their prices go down and it becomes difficult for farmers to earn a living. To keep the farmers afloat, the U.S. government has been paying farmers subsidies for decades. Doing this gives farmers more money than they would otherwise earn from their crops and sets up a minimum price for the cost of crops. In some cases, the government actually pays farmers *not* to plant crops.

Those who agree with the subsidy program believe it makes the economy fair, by making sure farmers are able to survive and receive a good price for the crops they grow, and by allowing them a fair chance to compete with the cheap crops that are imported from other countries. Opponents of farm subsidies say exactly the opposite. They feel subsidies are not fair and that they eliminate the possibility of a truly free market of the type on which the United States was built. Despite the long-standing controversy over the use of farm subsidies, it is unlikely that the government will repeal them

Farming is an important part of the U.S. economy. To help ensure farmers stay in business, the government gives many of them financial subsidies to increase or decrease production. Above, farmer Randy Floyd stands on his farm in Seagraves, Texas, in 2004. Between 1999 and 2004, he received subsidies totaling more than $250,000.

in the near future. In the meantime, the U.S. Congress has created a federal program where excess crops can be given to poorer countries, thus helping them and U.S. farmers.

EQUAL ACCESS TO HEALTH CARE

Even when people have health insurance, paying for surgeries and other treatments can cost an enormous amount of money. For those who do not have health insurance, medical care and prescription drugs may be impossible to afford.

Most people think of the United States as the most powerful and enlightened nation in the world, but when it comes to providing fair and universal health care to all its citizens, the United States lags far behind many other nations. In fact, it is the only industrialized country in the world that does not provide guaranteed access to health care to all of its people as a basic right of citizenship. The Universal Declaration of Human Rights, a founding document of the United Nations that was drafted by former U.S. First Lady Eleanor Roosevelt, states that all of the people in the world have "the right to a standard of living adequate for the health and well-being of himself and of his family, including food, clothing, housing and medical care. . . ." Despite the fact that the United Nations considers basic health care a major right of all people, the United States has not yet implemented a universal medical care system.

Every four years, when politicians campaign to become president of the United States, health care becomes a key issue. Leading up to the 2008 election, Democratic candidates Hillary Rodham Clinton and Barack Obama agreed that many changes were needed in the health-care system, but spent a large part of the Democratic primary campaign arguing over what type of health-care system they would set up if elected president. Despite the attention paid to health care, however, it will likely be years before any kind of universal system like that enjoyed in Europe and Canada will be established. Until then, many people would argue that the U.S. health-care system is unfair to some citizens. As Clinton, Obama, and Republican challenger John McCain noted, in many cases those who are employed and who can afford copays (small payments from the insured that are combined with payments from companies that provide medical insurance) and out-of-pocket expenses are able to get the best in medical treatment.

Although the United States does not have a system of health care that covers all its citizens equally, its people are fortunate not to face many of the medical problems, such as tuberculosis and sleeping sickness, that kill many people each year in underdeveloped nations in Africa and Asia.

Many people believe that the United States's health-care system is unfair, and it became a key topic in the 2008 presidential campaigns. Above, Democratic presidential candidate Senator Hillary Clinton (D-NY) discusses her plan to overhaul the health-care system at a rally in Des Moines, Iowa, in 2007.

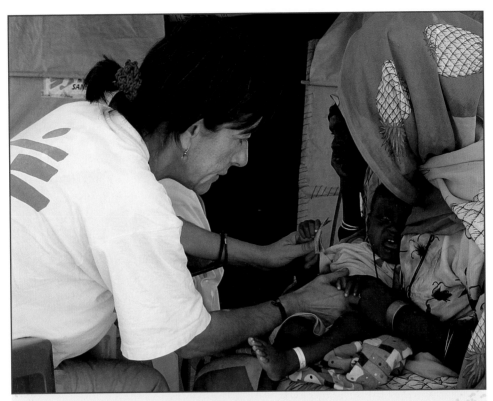

The goal of Doctors Without Borders is to have fair and equal health systems for people in all countries. Above, Dr. Mercedes Garcia examines a child in northern Darfur in 2005. Dr. Garcia and nurse Pilar Bauza, both members of Doctors Without Borders, were kidnapped in late 2007 by armed men in Somalia while they were on their way to treat malnourished children. They were released unharmed a week later in early 2008.

To try to provide medical treatment for poverty-stricken people, an international organization called Doctors Without Borders provides health care wherever people are suffering. In addition to giving direct medical treatment, Doctors Without Borders also speaks out in favor of fair and equal health systems for people in all countries of the world. One of the organization's most recent missions has been in the African nation of Kenya. After controversial elections took place in

December 2007, widespread violence erupted in Kenya. Representatives from Doctors Without Borders set up treatment centers in the affected areas. There, they tended to people who were wounded in the civil unrest while also continuing an ongoing program to vaccinate people against diseases such as measles and meningitis.

ECONOMIC FAIRNESS

For centuries, philosophers and economists have debated the best way to bring equality and fairness to the economies of the world and its individual nations. In the United States and many parts of Europe, capitalism has been the favored economic system. Under capitalism, businesses compete against one another in a free market, and the government does not regulate the way the economy works. Companies succeed or fail based on their own merits. Supporters of capitalism argue that giving all businesses an equal chance to compete is the fairest system possible. Others, however, believe that capitalism favors the rich, who, unlike the poor, can afford to own profitable businesses, while the working class is forced to labor in those businesses just to survive.

In the mid-nineteenth century, an economic theory called Marxism was developed by philosophers Karl Marx and Friedrich Engels. It suggested that the state, or government, should control all factories and property, doling out economic benefits to citizens according to their need. Marxists believed that this would be the fairest way to structure the economy, because, in theory, it would prevent any one group of people from becoming rich by exploiting the work of others. In reality, however, Marxist systems failed—they still had rich people who received many privileges, while the poor people of the lower classes did much of the work.

Politicians and citizens have argued for decades that the United States needs to find better ways to make sure that its economic policies treat all groups of people fairly. They believe that taking certain actions, such as raising the minimum

Karl Marx, pictured here in the mid- to late 1800s, developed the political philosophy of Marxism with Friedrich Engels in the mid-nineteenth century, thinking it would be the fairest way to structure the economy.

wage, can help spread the available money from the rich to the poor by shifting wealth from the top to the bottom of society. Yet, others argue that giving money to the poor is inherently unfair and only makes the poor dependent on the government to improve their economic condition. Finding a way to bring about social justice—to give all people equal opportunities to acquire equal wealth—is one of the key issues being debated by world leaders today.

EQUAL OPPORTUNITY

The civil rights movement of the 1960s resulted in the passage of laws that guaranteed equal rights to women and minorities. However, it remained to be determined how the U.S. government would actually provide a level playing field where people who had historically been excluded from certain jobs and places of education would have equal access to them. One way to provide equal opportunity is known as affirmative action. It was first mentioned on record in the Civil Rights Act of 1964, which was signed into law by President Lyndon B. Johnson. Affirmative action refers to steps that may be taken, such as the imposition of racial quotas, to force businesses and other institutions to accept or hire larger numbers of minorities.

Affirmative action first became a controversial public issue in the early 1970s, as colleges and businesses took steps to overturn racism and sexism, such as setting aside a certain number of slots for minorities to fill or giving preference to these job applicants even if they were not as fully qualified as other candidates. Since then, affirmative action has remained a hotly debated issue. While those who favor it argue that it makes the economy and the educational environment fair by working to erase the effects of past discrimination, opponents say that discriminating against the majority (in general, white males) is no fairer than it is to discriminate against minorities.

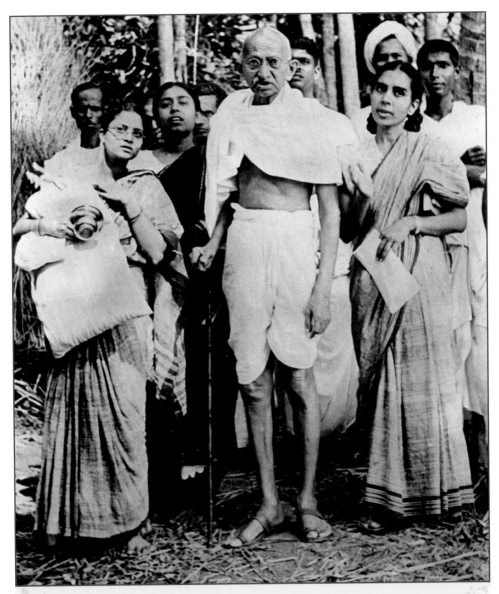

Mohandas Karamchand Gandhi, seen here in 1946 during his tour of Bengal province, worked to bring fairness and equality to all through peaceful means. He led a nonviolent campaign for India's independence from England and fought for equal rights for Untouchables, people of the lowest class based on the traditional Indian caste system.

Equal opportunity has been slow in becoming a reality, but progress has been made. One by one, minority businesspeople, academics, politicians, and athletes have broken through barriers—winning positions in traditional all-white institutions—and paved the way for others to follow. One dramatic example of this was the election of Barack Obama as the first African-American president of the United States on November 4, 2008.

Activists also promoted equal opportunity in other parts of the world. In India in the 1930s and 1940s, for example, Mohandas Gandhi, an Indian lawyer who led a nonviolent campaign to win India's independence from England, fought to win equal rights for the so-called Untouchables, who were traditionally considered the lowest members of a society based on a strict caste system. By the 1960s, India abolished the caste system, and, despite continued discrimination, the Untouchables became official members of Indian society.

The efforts of activists such as Lech Walesa, Martin Luther King Jr., Mohandas Gandhi, and the members of the American Indian Movement have gradually helped make the world a fairer place. They've also laid the groundwork for future generations to receive fair and equal treatment under the law.

HONESTY IN HISTORY

When a man lies, he murders some part of the world.

—Rospo Pallenberg and John Boorman, filmmakers,
in the screenplay for Excaliber *(1981)*

s the saying goes, "Honesty is the best policy." Even if most of us like to think of ourselves as honest, we may also think that dishonest people sometimes get ahead where honest people fail. History is full of incidents where people have lied to one another. But there are also plenty of times when people were brave enough to stand up and tell the truth. What follows is a look at honesty through history.

FREE SPEECH AND FREE PRESS

The First Amendment to the U.S. Constitution guarantees all American citizens the right to free speech and a free press. This freedom allows people to speak out honestly for what they believe in and shields them from certain kinds of lies because some forms of speech are not protected under the First Amendment. Lying under oath in a court of law (perjury), for example, is not protected as free speech. People who lie in court cannot justify their behavior by arguing that the First Amendment allows them to say whatever they like. Similarly, the Constitution does not allow people to lie if doing so can hurt others—for instance, it is against the law to shout "Fire!" when there is no fire in a crowded theater because it could cause chaos that might put people in danger.

The First Amendment also promises that people can tell the truth, even when others wish to keep them quiet. One landmark case regarding honesty and the First Amendment

GALILEO: BEING DISHONEST TO SAVE ONE'S LIFE

Nicolaus Copernicus (1473–1543) was a Polish astronomer who learned that, contrary to popular belief at the time, the Earth revolved around the Sun, instead of vice versa. This discovery ran counter to the tenets of the Catholic church, which was based on the premise that the Earth—and the human beings living on it—had been created by God as the center of the universe. Although knowledge of Copernicus's theory spread through Europe during his lifetime, it was not until after his death that later scientists, including Italian astronomer Galileo Galilei (1564–1642), were publicly attacked for believing in something that threatened the position of the church.

During Galileo's life, the Inquisition—a movement that sought to purify the Catholic Church and eliminate heretics (people who believed things that went against the church's teachings)—was in full swing. In 1633, the leaders of the Inquisition informed Galileo that he could either recant, or take back, his assertion that the Earth moves around the Sun or he would be put to death. By this time, Galileo was 70 years old and in poor health. To save his life, he denied the theory he knew to be true, saying: "I, Galileo Galilei ... abjure with sincere heart and unfeigned faith, I curse and detest the said errors and heresies [referring to Copernicus's theory]. And I swear that for the future I will neither say nor assert in speaking or writing such things as may bring upon me similar suspicion." Galileo was forced to tell a lie in order to save his life. In 1992, Pope John Paul II corrected a 350-year-old wrong by saying that the church was mistaken in silencing Galileo.

involved the Pentagon Papers. In 1971, journalist Daniel Ellsberg published secret documents he had uncovered that concerned the United States' policies in the Vietnam War. *The New York Times* printed Ellsberg's account of these documents, and the U.S. government responded by claiming that allowing any more of the Pentagon Papers to be published would cause "injury to the defense interests of the United States." The U.S. Supreme Court ruled against the government, permitting the *Times* to continue publishing the documents.

MUCKRAKERS

Working and living conditions in cities during the early part of the twentieth century were often deplorable. People were packed into tiny apartments, sometimes with whole families living in single rooms. Factories were dirty and not climate-controlled, and financial and legal institutions were corrupt. Between 1890 and 1914, an investigative journalism movement researched many of these problems and exposed them to the public in an attempt to drum up support for finding solutions. These journalists were called muckrakers, a name they received from President Theodore Roosevelt, who criticized them and gave a speech comparing them to a character called a muckraker in author John Bunyan's book *Pilgrim's Progress*. In the book, the muckraker was a person who "could look no way but downward with the muck-rake in his hands."

Among the most famous of the muckrakers were Ida Tarbell, who examined the lives of women and laborers; writer Upton Sinclair, who exposed conditions in slaughterhouses and oil businesses; and photojournalist Jacob Riis, who tried to help those living in poverty. Despite President Roosevelt's condemnation and the opposition of powerful businesspeople, the muckrakers were successful in bringing about a huge number of reforms between 1900 and 1915. These included child labor laws, pure food and drug legislation, penal system reforms, workers' compensation laws, and the

Journalist Upton Sinclair, seen here in 1906, blew the whistle on the unsanitary conditions of the meatpacking industry in his classic book, *The Jungle*. The public then demanded reforms in the industry.

conservation of natural resources. By telling the truth about American society and business, the muckrakers were able to help improve conditions for all people in the United States.

WHISTLE-BLOWERS

Whistle-blowers are people who publicly expose corruption and other forms of wrongdoing by business or government. In choosing to tell the truth about powerful corporations and governmental officials, the whistle-blowers risk retaliation that can cause them to lose their jobs and ruin their reputations. To try to protect whistle-blowers and the truths they tell, the Senate passed the Federal Employee Protection of Disclosures Act in 2006. This law strengthened protections for federal employees who expose corruption or problems in government policy.

Among the most famous whistle-blowers in U.S. history is Whittaker Chambers. During the 1940s, when the House of Representatives' Un-American Activities Committee was trying to expose Communists in the government, Chambers accused a man named Alger Hiss, who worked for the State Department, of belonging to the Communist Party in the United States. According to Chambers, Hiss was not a spy; instead, he was infiltrating the U.S. government in order to promote the interests of Russia, against which the United States was then pitted in a Cold War. Hiss denied the charges, but eventually, Chambers was able to prove his allegations by producing documents Hiss had stolen from the State Department to give to Russia. Before Hiss's involvement with the Communists was finally proven, many people viciously criticized Chambers. Despite this opposition, he chose to tell the truth, even though his own reputation (as an admitted former Communist) was harmed.

Another famous whistle-blower was the Russian scientist Andrei Sakharov. As part of the team that developed the Soviet Union's first hydrogen bomb, Sakharov had a close-up view of the arms race between the United States and Soviet

Union, in which both sides vied to build more and better nuclear weapons. In 1953, Sakharov began to feel that there were "moral problems inherent in [his] work" and decided to share with the world his opinion that nuclear weapons were a terrible danger. Starting in the late 1950s, Sakharov wrote papers and letters, telling the truth about the hazards of nuclear weapons and arguing in favor of a ban on nuclear testing. In 1975, he was awarded the Nobel Peace Prize for his work. Five years later, when he denounced the Soviet invasion of Afghanistan, he was sent into internal exile in the city of Gorky (which, at that time, was closed to foreigners). He was forced to remain there for seven years before he was allowed to return to Moscow.

Andrei Sakharov, shown here giving a speech in 1999, spoke out often about the dangers of nuclear weapons while exposing important truths to the public.

Perhaps the most famous whistle-blowers in the United States are journalists Bob Woodward and Carl Bernstein, who exposed the Watergate scandal that brought down Richard Nixon's presidential administration in the 1970s. Writing in *The Washington Post*, Woodward and Bernstein showed that the Republican Nixon administration had been involved in a June 1972 break-in at the Democratic campaign headquarters in the Watergate Hotel in Washington, D.C. The burglars were trying to tap the campaign office's phones and obtain any information that might help incumbent President Richard Nixon win the upcoming presidential election. Woodward and Bernstein's articles traced the planning of the break-in all the way to the White House. In 1974, Nixon was forced to resign in disgrace from the presidency.

DISHONESTY IN DEALINGS WITH NATIVE AMERICANS

From the first contact Europeans had with Native Americans, dishonesty prevailed. Broken treaties and agreements signed under false pretenses stripped the Native Americans of their land and independence. By the twentieth century, only a tiny fraction of the natives who had once lived in America were still alive, and many of these people were forced to live on reservations where the government controlled what cultural activities they took part in and what language they spoke.

When Native Americans began to fight for their civil rights in the 1960s, they formed groups such as the American Indian Movement (AIM) to protest the way the U.S. government had treated native peoples for centuries. In 1972, AIM and several other Native American activist groups carried out a protest called the Trail of Broken Treaties, intended to expose the truth about U.S. government treatment of native people throughout U.S. history. The protesters traveled to Washington, D.C., where they published a 20-point position paper outlining the various treaties the United States had

TELLING THE TRUTH EVEN IN THE FACE OF DEATH

Unlike Galileo, many people throughout history have refused to lie or deny their beliefs in order to save their lives. One of the most famous of these people was Joan of Arc (1412–1431). As a French teenager during the Hundred Years' War between England and France, Joan believed that she had experienced visions of God telling her that she would help France resist the English invasion of their land and bring France's King Charles VII to his rightful throne. After leading the entire French army in battle when she was just 17 years old, Joan was captured by the English and accused of heresy for claiming to have spoken directly to God. If she chose to lie and deny her belief in her own visions, Joan might have saved her life, but she refused to be dishonest and was convicted of heresy. She was burned at the stake in 1431, when she was just 19.

made and broken and how the government should provide reparations (payments) to try to make up for its treatment of the Native Americans. By publicly exposing the truth about how whites had treated native peoples, AIM and the other groups helped win support for their cause from Americans of all walks of life.

TELLING THE STORY OF MIGRANT WORKERS

During the Great Depression that began in the United States in 1929, after the stock market crashed and banks and businesses began to fail, many people lost their jobs, homes, and land. Among these people was the father of Cesar Chavez.

Cesar Chavez was the descendant of Mexican immigrants who lived in the American Southwest. After his father lost the land the Chavez family had owned since the 1880s, the family moved around the Southwest, working as laborers on farms and in vineyards. When he grew up, Chavez continued

Sir Thomas More (1478–1535) was another person who chose death over dishonesty. An English lawyer who served in the court of King Henry VIII of England, More was arrested when he refused to attend the coronation of Anne Boleyn, the woman Henry VIII had divorced his first wife, Catherine of Aragon, to marry. Refusing to go to the coronation was an act of treason. A commission acting on behalf of the king told More that he would have to state that he believed Parliament had the right to make Anne Boleyn the legitimate queen of England—a claim with which he did not agree. When he refused to swear to something he believed was untrue, More was sentenced to death. He was beheaded in July 1535. Like Joan of Arc, More refused to go against his beliefs to save his life, believing that the truth was more important than survival.

to work in orchards. There, he met a labor organizer named Fred Ross in 1952. Chavez joined Ross and became a full-time organizer, dedicated to promoting better treatment for farmworkers. Because many of these workers were not American citizens, their employers could make them work long hours for little pay, and there was not much they could do to protest. Chavez wanted to help migrant workers, both those who were citizens and those who were not, to win fair treatment from their employers.

Chavez exposed the truth about the migrants' working conditions and established the National Farm Workers Association (NFWA). Thanks to Chavez's efforts, the American public became aware of the plight of migrant workers and supported boycotts against grape growers that were led by Chavez and his fellow activists. Over time, farms and other agricultural interests were forced to provide better working conditions for migrants and to recognize their rights.

Cesar Chavez (*middle, with sign*) brought the plight of migrant workers to the attention of the American public and fought for them to have better working and living conditions. Here, Chavez walks with fellow activist Coretta Scott King (*left*) in New York City around 1973 to boycott unfair practices in lettuce farming. The two leaders show how activists can work together to bring more attention to a cause.

TELLING THE TRUTH ABOUT POLITICAL CORRUPTION

The details of the Watergate scandal exposed by journalists Bob Woodward and Carl Bernstein were, in part, uncovered because of the honesty of some of the people who had played a role in the Nixon administration during the cover-up of the Watergate break-in. One of these people was Alexander Butterfield, who served as deputy assistant to the president during the scandal. Because he was in charge of security for the White House, Butterfield had organized the installation of a secret taping system that recorded conversations in the White House. In 1973, he was called to testify before Congress about the Watergate scandal, and he was asked whether meetings that took place at the White House had been recorded. Although he knew that this was "the one thing that the President would not want revealed," Butterfield chose to tell the truth and admit that conversations had, in fact, been taped. Congress was then able to subpoena (have a court order the inclusion of evidence) these recordings and prove that the Nixon administration had been involved in Watergate.

Another person involved in Watergate who told the truth was John Dean, a lawyer who had served as counsel to

DISHONESTY JUSTIFIED: THE UNDERGROUND RAILROAD

During the years leading up to the American Civil War, a network of people who believed slavery was wrong sprang up to help slaves from the Southern states escape to freedom in the Northern states and Canada. This network was known as the Underground Railroad, and it was believed to be responsible for helping 100,000 slaves escape from the South between 1810 and 1850.

Lending slaves a hand required those involved to lie about what they were doing, since helping slaves get away from their owners was illegal. If slave catchers—people hired by slave owners to search for and return escaped slaves—questioned people who worked with the Underground Railroad, they had no choice but to lie in order to protect the runaways. Interestingly, a large number of the people who worked with the Underground Railroad were Quakers, members of a Christian denomination that abhors dishonesty. George Washington complained in 1786 that one of his slaves ran away with the help of a "society of Quakers, formed for such purposes." Despite their aversion to lying, these Quakers and their fellow "conductors" on the Underground Railroad chose to lie rather than betray the trust of the fugitive slaves or their own consciences.

U.S. President Richard Nixon gives his resignation speech on August 8, 1974 in a TV broadcast. Nixon's resignation was a humbling example of the importance of telling the truth.

President Nixon. Once the break-in had come to light and the administration took steps to cover up the White House's involvement, Dean stepped forward to tell Nixon that the decision to lie about the incident was causing "a cancer on the presidency." The administration ignored his advice, and Dean was eventually fired. Dean chose to continue to tell the truth, however, and went public with the information he knew about the White House's role in the burglary and cover-up. He testified before Congress and told the investigators that Nixon was guilty of helping to cover up the scandal. This was despite the fact that Dean himself was sent to prison for the role he played in the earlier days of the cover-up.

Oliver North was another government official who told the truth about his own involvement in a political scandal. North was a lieutenant colonel in the Marines who played a role in the Iran-Contra affair of the 1980s. The Iran-Contra scandal was a complicated arrangement in which members of the U.S. government sold weapons to Iran in order to obtain money to aid the Contra movement of rebels who were rising up against Nicaraguan dictator Manuel Noriega. When the scandal became public in 1986, North was fired by President Ronald Reagan's administration. A year later, North testified about his involvement in the affair, honestly admitting that he had lied to Congress in the past about whether or not he had committed the acts of which he was accused. He was put on trial and convicted of obstruction of justice, although his conviction was later overturned.

6 HONESTY AND FAIRNESS TODAY

It is not fair to ask of others what you are unwilling to do yourself.

—Eleanor Roosevelt (1884–1962), former U.S. First Lady

Although there are temptations all around us that make us think life would be easier if we cheated on tests or lied to get our way, not everyone succumbs to these temptations. What follows are a few profiles of modern-day heroes of honesty and fairness.

CRAIG KIELBURGER: FIGHTING UNFAIR CHILD LABOR

When he was 12 years old in 1995, Canadian Craig Kielburger read an article in the newspaper about another 12-year-old boy, named Iqbal Masih, who had recently been murdered in Pakistan for speaking out against poor working conditions for children in the carpet-making industry. Kielburger saw Masih as a hero, someone who had died fighting for what he believed in. Kielburger also learned from Masih's story that one person—even a young person—could help change the world.

Kielburger went on a trip through South Asia with a Canadian human rights advocate. There, he saw children working under terrible conditions, just as Iqbal Masih had described. When he got home, Kielburger wrote a book about his trip, called *Free the Children*. He also started a charitable foundation with some of his friends. Like Kielburger's book, it was called Free the Children, and none of its leaders was over the age of 18.

Kielburger's organization was funded through bake sales, car washes, and other activities that school groups use to raise money. The kids of Free the Children used the money to build more than 300 rural schools and rehabilitation centers in developing nations for children who had been held as

Canadian Craig Kielburger first made media headlines as a 12-year-old child labor crusader traveling through Asia. In 2007, he posed with students of a new school he helped build in Nairobi, Kenya. His Free the Children organization has more than a million supporters in 45 countries.

THE GIRAFFE PROJECT: CELEBRATING PEOPLE WHO DO THE RIGHT THING

In 1982, an organization called the Giraffe Project was created. The Giraffe Project celebrates the lives and accomplishments of so-called giraffes: people who choose to "stick their necks out" in order to do what is right and to promote the common good.

The "giraffes" are people honored for the work they do, whether it involves child labor, poverty, environmental issues, gang violence, or some other problem. The Giraffe Project asks two questions when it considers declaring someone a giraffe. These are: 1) Is there significant risk involved in what this person has done? and 2) Is it for the common good? Although many people work on useful projects or for good causes, what makes "giraffes" unique is that they face some sort of danger or risk of retribution for doing what they do.

Since its founding in 1982, the Giraffe Project has named more than 900 people as giraffes. Visit the project's Web site, www.giraffe.org, to read the inspiring stories and biographies of past giraffes.

slaves or exploited in other ways. Thanks to Kielburger and his group's efforts, countless children around the world have been freed or kept out of the child labor system.

WINFRED REMBERT JR.: INTEGRITY IN THE FACE OF GANG VIOLENCE

In 1987, Winfred Rembert Jr. was 11 years old and living with his family in New Haven, Connecticut. Local gang members tried to persuade Rembert to sell drugs for them, but he refused. Four years later, when he was 15, gang members approached him again and tried to get him to sell drugs. Once more, he said no.

Then, when he was 16, Rembert was playing basketball in his backyard when someone came by and told him that his younger brother Edgar had been beaten up by gang members. When Rembert ran to help his brother, one of the gang members tried to shoot Edgar, but Rembert was able to jump in and push him out of the way. Rembert was shot in the stomach.

Fortunately, he survived, and while he was in the hospital, he told a reporter, "I think he [the gang member] shot me to make a point to the neighborhood that you can't say no to them." Although it took two operations, Rembert recovered from the shooting. Meanwhile, the gang member who shot him was arrested.

Rembert had stood up for what he believed in, even when his very life was at stake. As he said, "You've just got to do what you think is right."

FAYE MCFADDEN AND HERBERT TARVIN: RETURNING FOUND MONEY

In January 1997, a Brinks truck loaded with $3.7 million overturned in Miami, Florida, and part of the money flew out into the street. Passersby who saw the money immediately ran over to try to take some for themselves, even though doing so was clearly dishonest.

To try to get the money back, the police gave people 48 hours to turn in the money without being arrested for stealing it. Only three people responded and returned the money they had found. Some $500,000 was still missing after the 48 hours had passed.

One of the people who returned the money was a firefighter who gave police a bag stuffed with around $330,000 (he never opened the bag, so he had no idea what it contained). The other two honest Miamians were 11-year-old Herbert Tarvin, who returned 85 cents, and Faye McFadden, a single mother who returned $19.53. Although police had hoped to get back larger sums of money, the incident demonstrated how easy it is for some people to give in to the temptation to be dishonest. Herbert Tarvin and Faye McFadden, however, felt that they had to do the right thing. As McFadden

RETURNING FOUND MONEY: THE STORY OF GULLI WIHLBORG'S WALLET

In 1963, when she was a teenager, Gulli Wihlborg went for a bike ride in Trelleborg, Sweden. While she was riding, she dropped her red leather wallet, which was full of pictures, money, and receipts. She never found it, and as the years passed, she pretty much forgot about it. She certainly never expected that it would one day be returned to her. That's why she was so surprised when her wallet showed up in the mail more than 40 years later, in January 2004.

The envelope that contained the wallet had been sent anonymously. Along with the wallet—and all of the money and other things it had contained when Wihlborg had lost it—the envelope held a note that read: "Dear Gulli, Never give up hope. Here is the wallet you dropped on Ostersjogatan [street] many years ago." Interestingly, whoever returned the wallet had had to do some research to find Wihlborg's current address, since she had moved 25 years ago from the place she had been living when she lost the wallet.

Wihlborg was very excited about getting her wallet back after so many years. She just wished that the honest person who returned it would come forward and let her know where the wallet had been for the past four decades.

explained it, "My heart wouldn't allow me to keep the money. It wasn't mine."

CYNTHIA COOPER: BLOWING THE WHISTLE ON WORLDCOM

Cynthia Cooper never intended to become a public whistle-blower. She just wanted to tell the truth to her boss in order to save the long-distance phone company, WorldCom, where she worked as an accountant.

In 2002, as she was going through WorldCom's accounting books, Cooper discovered that extensive fraud had been going on. By the time the scandal was fully exposed, the fraud that had been committed amounted to $9 billion. Five WorldCom executives were proven guilty and went to prison. When she noticed the fraud, Cooper wrote internal memos to let her superiors know what was going on, hoping that they could take action to fix the situation before the fraud was revealed publicly and threatened the existence of the company. Cooper's role might have gone no further than writing memos, but a member of the U.S. Congress leaked her memos to the press. That threw Cooper into the public spotlight as the woman who brought down WorldCom.

Although Cooper was uncomfortable with her role as a whistle-blower, she said that she would have done what she did again because she believed it was important to be honest. As she put it, when she discovered the fraud scandal, "I really found myself at a crossroads where there was only one right path to take. . . . It's important to be able to dig down and find your courage, which isn't always so easy."

SHERRON WATKINS: BLOWING THE WHISTLE ON ENRON

In 2001, the American energy company Enron went bankrupt amid charges of accounting scandals. In part, Enron's problems were exposed by a woman named Sherron Watkins, who was Enron's vice president of corporate development. Like Cynthia Cooper, Watkins did not intend to become a public figure or to destroy the company she worked for. She had hoped to save the company from the problems that she knew could bring it down if they were exposed publicly.

Watkins had worked at Enron for almost 10 years when she decided to send her boss, Kenneth Lay, a seven-page letter that informed him about fraudulent practices in the company's accounting. She wrote, "I am incredibly nervous that we will implode in a wave of accounting scandals." Watkins had no intention of being a whistle-blower. In fact, she wrote to Lay warning him that there might be whistle-blowers within the company who would expose the fraud to the public. She did not consider herself one of them.

Five months passed from the time Watkins wrote to Lay until the time when her letter was made public. All the while, Watkins continued to work at Enron. She says that once the scandal went public and put Enron on a downward spiral toward its ultimate bankruptcy, she was treated as an outcast at the office. Despite feeling uncomfortable around her colleagues, she knew she had done what was right. Her husband said he was proud that she had been a "team player."

FRANK SERPICO EXPOSES POLICE CORRUPTION

During the mid-twentieth century, police did not always operate according to the law. In some places, such as New York City, many cops were corrupt and took bribes from criminals to ignore their illegal activities. Often, even those police officers who were not corrupt themselves looked the other way when their fellow cops engaged in illegal actions. One person who chose to be honest and to expose police corruption was New York police officer Frank Serpico.

Frank Serpico became a policeman in 1960. Even as the cops around him took bribes and kickbacks from criminals, Serpico remained honest and refused to be dragged into the criminal underworld. In April 1970, *The New York Times* published a report that accused police of making millions of dollars every year by accepting bribes and other forms of payments from the Mafia and drug dealers. Serpico was one of the contributors to this report.

In October 1971, the Knapp Commission investigated the charges of police corruption. Serpico testified before this commission, saying, "The problem is that the atmosphere does not yet exist in which honest police officers can act without fear of ridicule or reprisal from fellow officers."

Serpico's fellow police officers were angry with him for testifying. While he was making an arrest a short time after

Frank Serpico (*center, with beard*) exposed corruption among his fellow police officers, which led to the Knapp Commission's formation. Here, Serpico sits with his attorney, Ramsey Clark, at the commission's investigation hearing in 1971 in New York City, where he testified.

he appeared before the Knapp Commission, he was shot in the face. Demonstrating their feelings about what he had done in exposing police corruption, the police did not try to help him. Fortunately, Serpico survived. He retired from the police force and lived overseas for a few years, not returning to New York until the 1980s. In 1973, his story was made into a film called *Serpico*, starring Al Pacino in the title role.

HONESTY IN SHARING LOTTERY WINNINGS

In the 1994 movie *It Could Happen to You*, Nicolas Cage stars as a New York police officer who offers to share a lottery ticket with a waitress when he realizes that he does not have enough money on him to give her a tip. He ends up winning the lottery and, against his wife's wishes, gives the waitress her rightful share of the winnings.

In real life, it did not happen quite that way, but it was nonetheless a great story of honesty in everyday life. In 1984, police officer Robert Cunningham from Dobbs Ferry, New York, was eating at Sal's Pizzeria, a restaurant he frequented. While he was joking around with the waitress—a woman named Phyllis Penzo whom he had known for years—he suggested that they buy a lottery ticket together, each choosing three of the six numbers. As in the movie, Cunningham said that he would share the lottery ticket with Penzo instead of giving her a tip. Penzo agreed, and they each picked three numbers.

They got lucky, winning a total of $6 million. Despite the fact that Cunningham could have tried to keep the fact that he won the lottery secret and not give Penzo her fair share, he split the winnings with her 50–50. And, unlike the movie, Cunningham's wife, Gina, was all for sharing the millions with Penzo. She said, "Hey, she picked three of those winning numbers. She gets her half of the pot."

HONESTY IN SPORTS: NATE HAASIS

In October 2003, at age 17, Nate Haasis was quarterback for Southeast High School in Springfield, Illinois. He was playing in a big game: If he completed a pass, he would set a passing record for his conference. When he made a 37-yard pass, he was thrilled. He had surpassed the record! But he soon found out that something was wrong. It turned out that Haasis's coach had made a deal with the coach of the opposing team. The Southeast High team would allow the other team to score, so that the ball would go back to Haasis, who could then have a chance to make his throw and break the record.

Quickly, people began to gossip about the incident, accusing the coaches of cheating. Even the local newspaper published an article about what had happened. Haasis knew he had to step forward and do what was right. He wrote a letter to the person in charge of his football conference. He said, "[I]t is my hope that this pass [the one that he broke the record with] is omitted from any conference records. . . . I would like to preserve the integrity and sportsmanship of a great conference for future athletes."

Nate Haasis had been honest in the face of heavy temptation: After all, if he had just kept silent, he might well have gone down in his local conference history as the player who broke the passing record. Instead, he chose to give up his accomplishment in order to preserve honesty in the sport he loved.

7
DEVELOPING YOUR CHARACTER

Good character is more to be praised than outstanding talent. Most talents are, to some extent, a gift. Good character, by contrast, is not given to us. We have to build it piece by piece—by thought, choice, courage and determination.

—*John Luther Long (1861–1927),*
American lawyer and writer

People grow through experience if they meet life honestly and courageously. This is how character is built.

—*Eleanor Roosevelt, former First Lady of the United States*

Imagine that you are at a department store buying yourself a new shirt. When you go up to the cashier, she accidentally gives you half off on the price, even though the shirt is not actually on sale. Do you tell her that she has made a mistake, or do you take your unfair discount and run?

Here is another scenario to consider: Your best friend goes out on a date and doesn't get a chance to do his math homework. In the morning, he asks to copy yours so he will not get in trouble with the math teacher. Do you let him use your work?

It can be difficult to figure out what the right thing is in some situations, especially when being dishonest or unfair would help someone you care about. In fact, there are actually times when you *should not* be completely honest. For example, say you had a bad weekend—you had to work and could not go to a friend's party, and you got in trouble with your parents for not washing the dishes after dinner. On Monday morning, someone asks you how your weekend was. Almost all of us would simply say something like, "Fine. How was yours?" Telling the whole truth in this situation would not only bore the other person, but would also unnecessarily burden him or her with having to hear about your problems. Having character means knowing when you should tell

WHAT THE ANCIENTS THOUGHT ABOUT CHARACTER

In ancient times, philosophers gave a great deal of thought to the idea of character. Ancient Greek philosopher Heraclitus (c. 540–480 B.C.) said, "Character is destiny." Many ancient thinkers believed that the fate of the entire world depended on the goodness of each individual person. As the Roman orator Cicero (106–43 B.C.) put it, "Within the character of the citizen lies the welfare of the nation." The ancient Greek Aristotle, one of the most famous philosophers of all time, said that character meant living what he called "the life of right conduct." This life included not just being good and fair when dealing with other people, but also doing the right thing when it came to yourself. In other words, Aristotle meant that you should do what is right even when you know that no one but you will ever know that you have done something wrong and that you should never try to talk yourself into doing something you know is wrong, even if you think it is for a "good reason."

the whole truth and when you should keep some things to yourself.

REASONS TO BE FAIR AND HONEST

In his book *20 Things I Want My Kids to Know,* author and former high school teacher Hal Urban lays out six reasons why it is good for us to be honest. The first is that being honest gives us peace of mind. When we lie, we have to be on constant guard to make sure no one finds out that we lied.

IS SCHOOL VIOLENCE RELATED TO A LACK OF CHARACTER EDUCATION?

In April 1999, two students at Columbine High School in Colorado opened fire, killing 12 people and injuring many others. In October 2006, a gunman entered an Amish schoolhouse in Pennsylvania and killed five girls. In April 2007, a student at Virginia Tech shot and killed 32 people before killing himself. Troubled by these kinds of incidents, the Conference on School Safety, organized by the federal government, considered the reasons for school violence and ways to prevent it. Craig Scott, who had survived the Columbine shooting, spoke before the conference, saying, "Incorporating character back into the education system is something my generation is desperately crying out for."

According to writer and motivational speaker Sandra Shelton, violence occurs when people do not know how to handle emotions and problems in their lives. In other words, people become violent when they have not learned good character. Shelton argues that the best way to prevent future incidents of school violence would be to incorporate character education into all American schools, led by adults who would mentor young people and help them learn how to act in fair, honest, and nonviolent ways. As Shelton put it, "The missing link in high school character education is the wise, personal, unique engagement for building positive, lasting relationships."

Being honest lets you live in peace, because you do not have to worry about keeping your story straight.

The second reason involves character and reputation. By being fair and honest, you develop habits that make you a good person—and other people will notice it. As a result, being honest can help you succeed.

Honesty also helps you in relationships. You cannot have a solid friendship or romantic relationship without being able to trust the other person. Being honest gives your relationships a solid basis on which to grow.

The fourth reason to be honest is the desire to be "whole." That is, honesty helps us become the very best person we can be, using all our potential. Without honesty, according to Urban, we will feel "empty" inside.

Good mental and physical health also depends on being fair and honest. Urban argues that being dishonest creates a state of tension in our bodies that can weaken the immune system and make us sick. Honesty keeps us healthy by keeping us free from guilt and worry.

Finally, being fair and honest allows us to live authentic lives. In other words, when we are honest, we are what we appear to be. We are not putting on a show or pretending to be something we are not.

DOS AND DON'TS OF BEING FAIR AND HONEST

How exactly do we go about being fair and honest? It is really quite simple. Keep an open mind and remain tolerant of other people and their points of view. Treat everyone equally, regardless of their race, religion, or ethnicity. Make sure to give everyone a fair chance and don't judge people before getting to know them. Play by the rules and don't take things that don't belong to you or deceive people into thinking you're something you're not. Don't cheat in school, work, or sports.

Being fair and honest also means that people must take only their fair share. Don't treat friends or family differently from strangers when it comes to giving out rewards or punishments. Don't take advantage of others or trick people into giving you things you don't deserve. Don't blame other people when you make a mistake.

STEPS TO DEVELOPING GOOD CHARACTER

The Character Council of Greater Cincinnati and Northern Kentucky provides information for schools and individuals about character education. According to its Web site, the organization has come up with six steps you can take to develop good character.

1. *Understand the quality:* To develop various character traits, such as honesty, fairness, or tolerance, you first need to understand what that trait (or quality) entails and how it is put into practice in daily life.
2. *Grasp its actions*: In this step, you learn how to describe a particular character trait and understand the way someone who possesses that trait behaves.
3. *Realize its benefits*: Understand what you can expect to gain from developing the traits of good character, including self-confidence, better relationships, and satisfaction with yourself.
4. *Practice its actions*: In this step, you act in the ways you described in Step 2. You develop habits in which you put the traits of good character, such as telling the truth and treating other people equally, to use.
5. *Encourage it in others*: Once you have begun to behave according to your new habits that reflect the traits of good character, you model that behavior for others to emulate. You praise other people when they show good character, and you treat those

around you as if you expect them to behave with fairness and honesty.

6. *Be encouraged*: Finally, you should let other people know that you are working to develop your character and ask them to give you encouragement and praise as you put your new habits into action.

TEACHING CHARACTER

As character education becomes part of more and more school programs, experts have come up with various methods for teaching young people to be honest and fair, and to demonstrate other traits associated with good character. Some say that character is best taught by having children *do* the things they should be doing. For example, if you intend to teach kids to be independent and responsible when it comes to doing their schoolwork, you make sure that they are held responsible for getting their work done and that they do not get unapproved help from their parents or other sources. Other experts say that you can teach character by drawing up lists of rules and behaviors that are either right or wrong, which young people can memorize and later apply to their own lives. Still others say that the best way to teach young people to have good character is by showing that you are a model of good character yourself, thereby providing others with a model for how they should behave.

In teaching character, it is also important to pay attention to what young people say and do. When a child says that something is unfair, it is an opportunity to discuss the right and wrong ways to treat people and to teach about compromise. Letting young people explain their opinions without judging or criticizing them is also an essential part of learning not to unfairly judge or put down others.

The biggest part of teaching character involves giving young people opportunities to do good things, things that show them that honesty and fairness are important in real life, not just as abstract concepts. Many communities have character-promoting organizations that provide ideas to help you develop your character. The Character Education Partnership (http://www.character.org) is a national organization for promoting character education in the United States. The Center for the 4th & 5th Rs (http://www.cortland.edu/character/) instructs educators on how to teach the character qualities of respect and responsibility just like they teach reading, writing, and arithmetic. The Josephson Institute of Ethics (http://josephsoninstitute.org/) publishes information obtained from surveys about how honest and fair people are. Goodcharacter.com is a Web site that provides young people with opportunities to help build their character, doing things such as volunteering to work with groups such as Habitat for Humanity or engaging in social activism to end child labor or promote human rights. Thanks to organizations and Web sites such as these, it is easy to find information that can help you develop your own character and become a model citizen who can serve as an example for others to follow.

A REPORT CARD ON THE ETHICS OF AMERICAN YOUTH

The Josephson Institute collects survey data to analyze how fair and honest Americans are. In October 2006, during National Character Counts Week, a time dedicated to promoting character education in schools and society, the Josephson Institute released a report card on ethics among young people in the United States. There was positive and negative news.

The positive news was that almost all of the young adults surveyed (98 percent) said that it was important for them to be a person with good character. While 83 percent said that it would not be worth it to lie because lying harms your character, 98 percent agreed with the statement, "Honesty and trust are essential in personal relationships." Most of those interviewed (82 percent) also said that they believed most of the adults in their lives were good examples of character, and that it is more important to be a good person than to be wealthy (89 percent).

However, there were some negative trends uncovered by the survey. Large portions of the young people questioned seemed to be very cynical about honesty in everyday life. Some 59 percent said that they agreed with the statement, "In the real world, successful people do what they have to do to win, even if others consider it cheating." Another 42 percent said that they agreed that people sometimes have to lie or cheat if they want to succeed. Plus, many young people admitted that they had lied or cheated themselves. Eighty-two percent said they had lied to a parent or guardian about something important over the last year.

Essentially, the Josephson Institute's study found that, while young people believe that good character is important philosophically, when it came down to real life, they were often willing to lie or behave unfairly if it would help them get ahead. The hope is that character education in schools will help young people learn not only to believe that fairness and honesty are right, but also to act on those beliefs.

GLOSSARY

bias Prejudice; a preference for something

bigotry Intolerance toward people who are different from you

caste system A hierarchy made up of different social classes into which people are born

Cold War A sustained conflict between nations over differing beliefs without actual military action

compromise The settlement of differences in which each side makes concessions so that everyone can agree

copay A fee paid by a patient that represents a portion of the cost of health care, the rest of which will be paid by insurance

doping Taking drugs or other substances in order to improve athletic performance

due process Formal legal proceedings to which all citizens have a right

forgery Falsely changing a document or signing someone else's name

guilds Associations of workers from different trades

heretics People who do not agree with the accepted religious beliefs

human growth hormone A natural substance found in the body that promotes the growth of muscle

hypocrite A person who says one thing but does another

hypothesis A belief about something that needs to be tested in order to be proven or disproven

impartial Fair; not biased

just Fair; upright

karma The belief that the way you behave will be reflected in what happens to you. If you do what is right, good things will happen; if you do wrong, bad things will happen

peer-reviewed Evaluated by experts in the same field

perjury Lying while under an oath to tell the truth, as in a court of law

plagiarism Using someone else's work without giving credit

racial profiling Using race, gender, or other factors to single people out for suspicion of criminal or other activity

reparations Payments designed to make up for unfair treatment in the past

reservations Parcels of land set aside for Native Americans to live on

royalties Payments received by an artist whenever his or her work is sold

stereotypes Beliefs or opinions about a group of people based on biased incorrect or incomplete assumptions

steroids Chemicals that contain hormones and can lead to muscle growth

subpoena A court order to submit a piece of evidence or for a witness to appear

subsidies Money given to help a group of people by supplementing their income

suffrage The right to vote

syllabary A table of written characters that function as an alphabet or basis for a language

BIBLIOGRAPHY

BOOKS

Lewis, Barbara A. *What Do You Stand For?* Minneapolis: Free Spirit Publishing, 1998.

Lickona, Thomas. *Character Matters*. New York: Touchstone Books, 2004.

——. *Educating for Character: How Our Schools Can Teach Respect and Responsibility*. New York: Bantam Publishers, 1991.

Urban, Hal. *20 Things I Want My Kids to Know*. Nashville, Tenn.: Thomas Nelson, 1992.

ARTICLES

"ACLU Sues Maryland State to Obtain Public Records Relating to Racial Profiling." American Civil Liberties Union. n.d. Available online. URL: http://www.aclu.org/racialjustice/racialprofiling/index.html. Accessed March 6, 2008.

Ackman, Dan. "The WorldCom We Hardly Knew." Forbes.com. June 26, 2002. Available online. URL: http://www.forbes.com/2002/06/26/0626topnews.html. Accessed March 6, 2008.

"Affirmative Action." *Stanford Encyclopedia of Philosophy*. March 4, 2005. Available online. URL: http://plato.stanford.edu/entries/affirmative-action/. Accessed March 6, 2008.

"The African-American Mosaic." Library of Congress. July 5, 2005. Available online. URL: http://www.loc.gov/exhibits/african/afam002.html. Accessed March 6, 2008.

American Indian Movement Grand Governing Council. "AIM-GGC Profile." American Indian Movement. n.d. Available online. URL: http://www.aimovement.org/ggc/index.html. Accessed March 6, 2008.

——. "The Trail of Broken Treaties." n.d. Available online. URL: http://www.aimovement.org/ggc/trailofbroken treaties.html. Accessed March 6, 2008.

Anderson, William, and Gene Callahan. "The Roots of Racial Profiling." Reason Online. August/September 2001. Available online. URL: http://www.reason.com/news/printer/28138.html. Accessed March 6, 2008.

The Andrei Sakharov Foundation. n.d. Available online. URL: http://asf.wdn.com/cgi/ASFdbs.pl?action=Linkview&link_res_doc=main.897342898.html. Accessed March 6, 2008.

"Asa Philip Randolph." AFL-CIO. 2008. Available online. URL: http://www.aflcio.org/aboutus/history/history/randolph.cfm?RenderForPrint=1. Accessed March 6, 2008.

Battista, John R., and Justine McCabe. "The Case for Single Payer, Universal Health Care for the United States." Connecticut Coalition for Universal Health Care. June 4, 1999. Available online. URL: http://cthealth.server101.com/the_case_for_universal_health_care_in_the_united_states.htm Accessed March 6, 2008.

Becker, Steve. "The Becker Sports Report." 2005. Available online. URL: http://sportssatirereport.com/2005_Articles/111_Mark_McGuire.shtml. Accessed March 6, 2008.

Bennett, William J. "Teaching the Virtues." School for Champions. March 9, 2003. Available online. URL: http://schoolforchampions.com/education/teaching_virtues.htm. Accessed March 6, 2008.

Block, Water. "Social Justice." LewRockwell.com. January 26, 2004. Available online. URL: http://www.lewrockwell.com/block/block37.html. Accessed March 6, 2008.

"A Brief Biography of Sequoyah." The Sequoyah Birthplace Museum. n.d. Available online. URL: http://sequoyahmuseum.org/SequoyahHistory.html. Accessed March 6, 2008.

"Building Character." Character Council of Greater Cincinnati and Northern Kentucky. 2000. Available online. URL: http://charactercincinnati.org/sixsteps.html. Accessed March 6, 2008.

"Cheating." KidsHealth. February 2007. Available online. URL: http://www.kidshealth.org/PageManager.jsp?dn=KidsHealth

&lic=1&ps=307&cat_id=20070&article_set=22054. Accessed March 6, 2008.

"Child Labor in Nineteenth-Century Literature." Enotes. February 11, 2008. Available online. URL: http://www.enotes.com/nineteenth-century-criticism/child-labor-nineteenth-century-literature/introduction?print=1. Accessed March 6, 2008.

Cline, Adrian H. "Teaching Children to Be Fair." DeSoto Schools. April 29. 2003. Available online. URL: http://www.desotoschools.com/Cline%2004.29.03.htm. Accessed March 6, 2008.

CNN Interactive. "Only two return money from overturned Brinks truck." U.S. News Story Page. January 13, 1997. Available online. URL: http://www.cnn.com/US/9701/13/briefs.pm/loose.change.html. Accessed March 6, 2008.

Cozzens, Lisa. "Brown v. Board of Education." Watson.org. 1995. Available online. URL: http://www.watson.org/~lisa/blackhistory/early-civilrights/brown.html. Accessed March 6, 2008.

Davis, Ronald L. F. "From Terror to Triumph: Historical Overview." *The History of Jim Crow.* Available online. URL: http://www.jimcrowhistory.org/history/overview.htm. Accessed March 6, 2008.

Democracy Now! "Worse Than Watergate: Former Nixon Counsel John Dean Says Bush Should Be Impeached." *The War and Peace Report.* April 6, 2004. Available online. URL: http://www.democracynow.org/2004/4/6/worse_than_watergate_former_nixon_counsel. Accessed March 6, 2008.

"Giraffe Heroes." Giraffe Heroes Project. Available online. URL: http://www.giraffe.org/hero.html. Accessed March 6, 2008.

Goodale, James C. "The First Amendment and Freedom of the Press." Issues of Democracy. February 1997. Available online. URL: http://usinfo.state.gov/journals/itdhr/0297/ijde/goodale.htm. Accessed March 6, 2008.

"Human Rights." U.S. Department of State. Available online. URL: http://www.state.gov/g/drl/hr/. Accessed March 6, 2008.

"Human Rights and Migrant Workers." *The Human Rights of Migrant Workers.* n.d. Available online. URL: http://www.pdhre.org/rights/migrants.html. Accessed March 6, 2008.

Jacobs, Jerrilyn. "Peacemaker Hero: Craig Kielburger." *Peacemaker Heroes.* Available online. URL: http://www.myhero.com/myhero/heroprint.asp?hero=c_kielburger. Accessed March 6, 2008.

Josephson Institute of Ethics. "What's the Big Deal About Cheating?" *Honor Above All: Character Counts.* 2004.

———. "2006 Josephson Institute Report Card on Ethics of American Youth." *Character Counts.* October 15, 2006. Available online. URL: http://www.josephsoninstitute.org/pdf/ReportCard_press-release_2006–1013.pdf. Accessed March 6, 2008.

Kennedy, Robert. "Cheating 101 for Private Schools." About.com: Private Schools. 2007. Available online. URL: http://privateschool.about.com/cs/forteachers/a/cheating.htm?p=1. Accessed March 6, 2008.

Kinsela, Paul. "101 wallets deliberately dropped in front of hidden cameras to test honesty." WalletTest.com. December 2006. Available online. URL: http://www.wallettest.com/Lost_Wallet_Test/Press_Release.html. Accessed March 6, 2008.

Knox, David. "Deception of Parents During Adolescence." BNET.com. Fall 2001. Available online. URL: http://findarticles.com/p/articles/mi_m2248/is_143_36/ai_82535331/. Accessed March 6, 2008.

Mark, Lois Alter. "Reality Check: Winning Personalities." EW.com. 2008. Available online. URL: http://www.ew.com/ew/article/0,,303110,00.html. Accessed March 6, 2008.

McCabe, Donald. "Cheating: Why Students Do It and How We Can Help Them Stop." *American Educator.* Winter 2001. Available online. URL: http://www.aft.org/pubs-reports/american_educator/winter2001/Cheating.html. Accessed March 6, 2008.

"Mitchell Report: The Lineup." The Smoking Gun. December 13, 2007. Available online. URL: http://www.thesmokinggun.

com/archive/years/2007/1213071mitchell1.html. Accessed March 6, 2008.

"Muckraking." Spartacus. Available online. URL: http://www. spartacus.schoolnet.co.uk/Jmuckraking.htm. Accessed March 6, 2008.

Munday, Bonnie. "How Honest Are You?" *Reader's Digest.* 2005. Available online. URL: http://www.readersdigest.ca/ mag/2005/05/honesty.html. Accessed March 6, 2008.

Nieves, Evelyn. "Our Towns: Jackpot: Two Lives Inspire Art." *The New York Times.* July 26, 1994. Available online. URL: http://query.nytimes.com/gst/fullpage.html?res=9507E4DF1 13EF935A15754C0A962958260. Accessed March 6, 2008.

PBS. "People & Events: Passage of the Fifteenth Amendment." *American Experience.* Available online. URL: http://www. pbs.org/wgbh/amex/grant/peopleevents/e_fifteenth.html. Accessed March 6, 2008.

Pellegrini, Frank. "Person of the Week: 'Enron Whistleblower' Sherron Watkins." *Time.* January 18, 2002. Available online. URL: http://www.time.com/time/printout/0,8816,194927,00. html. Accessed March 6, 2008.

Pinker, Steven. "The Moral Instinct." *The New York Times.* January 13, 2008. Available online. URL: http://www. nytimes.com/2008/01/13/magazine/13Psychology-t.html?_ r=1&oref=slogin. Accessed March 6, 2008.

Quinn, Ryan. "Why the Silence?: Athletes Need to Speak out About Sports Doping." *Outsports.* 2005. Available online. URL: http://www.outsports.com/columns/2005/ 0209quinndoping.htm. Accessed March 6, 2008.

"Racism." Anti-Defamation League. 2001. Available online. URL: http://www.adl.org/hate-patrol/racism.asp. Accessed March 6, 2008.

"Rain of Cash in Car Crash Tempts Poor from Miami." *The New York Times.* January 12, 1997. Available online. URL: http://query.nytimes.com/gst/fullpage.html?res= 9C00E4DB1538F931A25752C0A961958260. Accessed March 6, 2008.

Rains, Craig. "Little Rock Central High: 40th Anniversary." Central High School. September 1997. Available online. URL: http://www.centralhigh57.org. Accessed March 6, 2008.

Rendall, Steve. "The Fairness Doctrine; How we lost it, and why we need it back." Fairness and Accuracy in Reporting. January/February 2005. Available online. URL: http://www.fair.org/index. Accessed March 6, 2008.

Ripley, Amanda. "Q&A: Whistle-Blower Cynthia Cooper." *Time*. February 4, 2008. Available online. URL: http://www.time.com/time/printout/0,8816,1709695,00.html. Accessed March 6, 2008.

Sanghavi, Darshak. "Detecting Doping in Sports." *International Herald Tribune*. October 4, 2007. Available online. URL: http://www.iht.com/bin/print.php?id=7751938. Accessed March 6, 2008.

"Sequoyah." About North Georgia. Available online. URL: http://ngeorgia.com/ang/Sequoyah(a.k.a._George_Gist). Accessed March 6, 2008.

"Serpico Testifies." *New York Magazine*. 2008. Available online. URL: http://nymag.com/news/articles/03/03/35th/crazedcity/crimes/1.htm. Accessed March 6, 2008.

Shah, Anup. "Racism." Global Issues.org. December 20, 2004. Available online. URL: http://www.globalissues.org/HumanRights/Racism,asp?p=1. Accessed March 6, 2008.

Shaver, Katherine. "Conference Addresses School Shootings." *The Washington Post*. October 11, 2006. Available online. URL: http://www.washingtonpost.com/wp-dyn/content/article/2006/10/10/AR2006101000124_pf.html. Accessed March 6, 2008.

Sheinin, Dave. "Baseball Has a Day of Reckoning in Congress." washingtonpost.com. March 18, 2005. Available online. URL: http://www.washingtonpost.com/ac2/wp-dyn/A4322–2005Mar17?language=printer. Accessed March 6, 2008.

Shelton, Sandra. "How Many School Shootings Will It Take for Us to 'Get It'?" SearchWarp.com. April 26, 2007. Available online. URL: http://searchwarp.com/swa151562.htm. Accessed March 6, 2008.

"Sportsmanship." KidsHealth. May 2005. Available online. URL: http://www.kidshealth.org/PageManager.jsp?dn= KidsHealth&lic=1&ps=107&cat_id=20459&article_set=27891. Accessed March 6, 2008.

"Stealing." KidsHealth. July 2006. Available online. URL: http:// www.kidshealth.org/PageManager.jsp?dn=KidsHealth&lic= 1&ps=307&cat_id=2008&article_set=22817. Accessed March 6, 2008.

"Teaching Your Child Tolerance." KidsHealth. December 2002. Available online. URL: http://www.kidshealth. org/PageManager.jsp?dn=KidsHealth&lic=1&ps=107&cat_ id=145&article_set=20864. Accessed March 6, 2008.

Thompson, Charles. "Plessy v. Ferguson: Harlan's Great Dissent." *Harlan's Great Dissent.* 1996. Available online. URL: http://www.law.louisville.edu/library/collections/harlan/ dissent. Accessed March 6, 2008.

United Nations. "Universal Declaration of Human Rights." 1998. Available online. URL: http://www.un.org/Overview/rights. html. Accessed March 6, 2008.

"Wallet Returned After 40 Years." BBC News. February 2, 2004. Available online. URL: http://newsvote.bbc.co.uk/mpapps/ pagetools/print/news.bbc.co.uk/2/hi/europe/3451857.stm. Accessed March 6, 2008.

Whalen, Robert G. "Hiss and Chambers: Strange Story of Two Men." *The New York Times.* December 12, 1948. Available online. URL: http://www.writing.upenn.edu/~afilreis/50s/ hiss-chambers-nyt.html. Accessed March 6, 2008.

White, Patricia. "To Be Totally Frank . . . Teaching the Complex Virtue of Honesty." *Philosophy of Education.* 1993. Available online. URL: http://www.ed.uiuc.edu/EPS/PES- Yearbook/93_docs/WHITE.HTM. Accessed March 6, 2008.

FURTHER RESOURCES

BOOKS

Anderson, Terry. *The Pursuit of Fairness: A History of Affirmative Action*. New York: Oxford University Press, 2005.

Kolomeisky, Dorothy. *All About You: A Course in Character for Teens*. Charleston, SC: Book Surge Publishing, 2007.

Myers, R.E. *Exploring Character*. Tucson, AZ: Good Year Books, 2006.

Newton, Cathy. *It Takes Character*. Nashville, TN: Incentive Publications, 2004.

WEB SITES

Center for the 4th & 5th Rs
http://www.cortland.edu/character/
This site provides character information and educational materials that are related to the writings of character expert Tom Lickona.

Character Development Group
http://www.charactereducation.com/
This site provides information and statistics on character and information on bringing character education to schools.

Character Education Network
http://www.charactered.net/
This site includes teaching materials and suggestions for ways to improve one's character.

Character Education Partnership
http://www.character.org/site/c.iplJKTOEJsG/b.3438707/
One of the world's premier character education organizations. It is recognized as a leader in the field and a foremost advocate for developing young people of good character and civic virtue.

GoodCharacter.com
http://www.goodcharacter.com/
This site provides teaching materials and activities to help people develop character.

The Josephson Institute: Character Counts!
http://charactercounts.org/
This site, run by the Josephson Institute of Ethics, explains the importance of character in society.

PICTURE CREDITS

INDEX

ABOUT THE AUTHOR AND SERIES CONSULTANTS

Tara Tomczyk Koellhoffer earned a degree in political science and history from Rutgers University. Today, she is a freelance writer and editor with more than 12 years of experience working on nonfiction books, covering topics ranging from social studies and biography to health and science. She has edited hundreds of books and teaching materials, including a history of Italy published by Greenhaven Press and the *Science News for Kids* series published by Chelsea House. She lives in Pennsylvania.

Series consultant **Dr. Madonna Murphy** is a professor of education at the University of St. Francis in Joliet, Illinois, where she teaches education and character education courses to teachers. She is the author of *Character Education in America's Blue Ribbon Schools* and *History & Philosophy of Education: Voices of Educational Pioneers*. She has served as the character education consultant for a series of more than 40 character education books for elementary school children, on the Character Education Partnership's Blue Ribbon Award committee recognizing K-12 schools for their character education, and on a national committee for promoting character education in teacher education institutions.

Series consultant **Sharon L. Banas** was a middle school teacher in Amherst, New York, for, more than 30 years. She led the Sweet Home Central School District in the development of its nationally acclaimed character education program. In 1992, Sharon was a member of the Aspen Conference, drafting the Aspen Declaration that was approved by the U.S. Congress. In 2001, she published *Caring Messages for a School Year*. She has been married to her husband, Doug, for 37 years. They have a daughter, son, and new granddaughter.